Descendants of Rajgród

LEARNING TO FORGIVE

Dear Richetla + Linda,
wishing you both peace
+ joy. —— Karen

A Memoir

KAREN L. KAPLAN

Descendants of Rajgród

LEARNING TO FORGIVE

Karen L. Kaplan

Manora Press

Manora Press

ISBN: 0692207619
ISBN 13: 9780692207611

To My Three Precious Angels - Max, Noah and Raquel,
The Joys of My Life.

To Bobby - My True Companion

CONTENTS

PROLOGUE

M y friend Ross, a psychotherapist, knew of a woman named Lea, who helped one of his patients improve in a remarkable way. I was eager to learn more about her because I wanted to live a more meaningful and happier life. I had been divorced since 2003, raising three children and searching to bring a sense of spirituality into my family home.

I have come to realize that there are no coincidences in life and that everything happens for a reason. So I was determined to understand how my upbringing had impacted my life and was no longer fearful or ashamed to dig deep and uncover my burdensome past; my father, a survivor of the Holocaust, had made life for my mother, brothers and me quite unbearable and I did not want to live with the effects any longer.

For the last ten years I've made it a practice to host all sorts of spiritual classes for friends and community members so in June of 2009, I invited Lea, a spiritual teacher and psychotherapist, into my home to address the topic of spirituality and healing. Lea was born and raised in a small mid-western town and she brought along her husband, Don, who grew up in the Appalachian mountains of Tennessee. Lea had a private practice, traveled and spoke throughout the country, and spent the winter months in Florida. She was sweet natured and humble, yet very confident as she spoke in my dining room to a packed room of over twenty five people.

Toward the end of her lecture, she said something that baffled me: "Your Jewish community has been through a long history of suffering and pain and you need to heal." Lea suggested that I can help plant the seed for this healing process right here in my home. The judgmental side of me set in quickly. What a bizarre comment, I thought, and then I wondered if she was sort of nuts. She grew up in an area where there were very few Jews and those in her area were not connected to the Jewish community. So how could she presume to know the needs of any Jews at all, let alone this Jewish area on the North Shore of Chicago.

Then she asked me to lead and sing a Hebrew prayer of peace. We all stood up in the room, held hands and I began to sing a popular prayer. Many in the circle joined in and sang.

Oseh shalom bimromav, hu ya ase shalom alenu v'al kol yisra'el, v'imru, Amen.

May the One who causes peace to reign in the high heavens let peace descend on us and on all Israel, and let us say, Amen.

Over time, I began reflecting on Lea's comments and I realized that just as all of us are affected in some way by our upbringing, the Jewish community today carries burdens from its long turbulent history. Several months later I began working with Lea and trying to make some sense of my past to help me create a brighter future.

I wrote this book because I went through a transformation. I unknowingly had been trapped in the pain and fears of my past and struggled throughout my life. Eventually I learned to live a happier life as I learned to let go of the negative feelings that had entrapped me. The process became a cathartic experience for me.

Tolstoy wrote: "Happy families are all alike, every unhappy family is unhappy in its own way." Mine was one of the unhappy ones. Throughout my life, I have experienced many conflicts from within my family and community that were challenging and life altering. These experiences have taxed my physical, mental and spiritual body and certainly could have hindered me from living a complete and meaningful life. Yet, these very occurrences—what I consider "life lessons" —have enabled me to grow and become a more authentic and fulfilled person. These life lessons have brought me closer to my life purpose.

I believe that we are all here for a purpose. Not everyone recognizes or understands his or her purpose. Some people go through life without ever finding meaning, and some, like me, search tirelessly until we find it. I had repeatedly encountered situations bearing the same schematic themes begging me to wake up and change. Once I realized that something needed to happen, if I was ever going to be happy, I began the search in earnest.

I had become a victim of life lessons that distorted my reality. I thought, felt and behaved according to this artificial foundation I created. Negative consequences resulted that I carried into my adult life and unknowingly passed on to my children.

I always thought I was a truth seeker until I discovered that I was hiding from the truth all along. I understand that not everyone will agree with my conclusions, but I've worked long and hard to reach an understanding about what I think is best for me and my Jewish community.

I willingly share my tumultuous childhood in hopes that anyone who has spent his or her entire life suffering and holding onto painful memories can learn to let them all go.

This book is also about helping my family heal, and by "family" I mean my tribe, my Jewish community. This book explores some of our deep-seated beliefs and fears that continue to make us feel like victims of the world and block our path to becoming a completely whole people who can live a more uplifting and authentic life. This book offers my insight into our collective way of thinking and provides an opportunity to elevate our level of awareness as a people.

Ultimately, this book is a tribute to my father, Arie Kaplan. Because of him, I delved deeper into myself so that I could heal, guide my children and share what I learned with my people. My dad, in spite of his weaknesses as a father and human being, enabled me to awaken to a more purposeful way of life.

ONE

The Proudest Moment

You will find as you look back upon your life that the moments
when you have really lived are the moments when you have done
things in the spirit of love.
-Henry Drummond

My sixteen-year-old son, Noah, was working on a high-school project and needed to interview a family member. He felt compelled to interview my father, Papa Arie, because he had survived the Holocaust. He wanted to share the personal plight of his grandfather's life with his classmates. Noah was excited and prepared a long list of questions; he also brought a tripod and video camera to tape the interview. Personally, I was bewildered at how simple it was for my son to sit down with my father and ask him personal questions about his past, I had never thought to ask. Nobody that I knew had ever asked their parents such questions. Living with a parent and never fully knowing the history of his childhood seemed awfully strange, yet it was the norm in my Jewish community. Many people of my parents' generation had kept their personal stories to themselves. They simply never discussed them. Eagerly anticipating the details of my father's childhood--and certainly very grateful for my son's boldness--I, too, was eager to begin the interview.

Papa Arie was eighty-seven years old at the time and hard of hearing, but quite alert and remarkably attentive to his surroundings. He was thin and stood fairly erect at five-foot-seven; over the years he had shrunk some. He still had a full head of hair, though his once dark-brown and satiny hair had turned gray. He was a remarkably handsome man when he was younger, and physically fit as well, since he avidly played volleyball, swam, and later in life walked every day. At eighty-seven he kept striving to stay in shape by walking in the malls when it was cold outside, or walking up and down his apartment hallway. My father was generally careful about eating right, veering away from foods high in fat or salt. He did not care much about sweets; instead, he enjoyed a fresh hot garlic and onion bagel or bialy with a piece of herring or other smoked fish to start his day. As he aged, the skin around his face had become thinner, and the age lines formed horizontal grooves on his forehead. Vertical lines between his brows were usually pronounced because he frowned quite a bit. His dark brown eyes appeared much smaller over the years as they sunk deep into his eye sockets. Conversing with my father had become a tiresome task, since it was necessary to lean in closely toward him, turning to one of his ears, and speaking slowly and loudly.

My father was noticeably uncomfortable being taped by Noah, but I assured him several times that the government would not find out about this recorded interview. Yet he seemed paranoid. We sat at my kitchen table and, because Noah couldn't make himself heard, I asked the questions from his long list. Surprisingly, my father began answering each question one by one, succinctly recalling the names and birth dates of his family members and details of their lives before World War II. Then I asked my father the details about the day his family died. He started to describe it, became agitated, and began to weep. Embracing him or showing him any sign of affection was not an option, so all I could do was simply watch him cry. I felt helpless as I witnessed his pain. My own tears came later, when I was alone.

"I don't vont to answer any more qvestions," he said in his Polish accent. "I'm done."

Noah was very respectful, but he decided to ask his grandpa one final question, which I repeated so my father could hear: "What was the proudest moment of your life?"

A plethora of events from our family's life cycle raced through my mind. Which moment would my father choose? After all, he is a survivor of the Holocaust and had miraculously emerged with a determination to pass on the ancient Jewish traditions and rituals of our people to his children. He married, fathered three children, and raised them in a strictly Jewish environment.

Would his proudest moment be his wedding day or the births of his three children? Or perhaps when his two sons became "Bnai Mitzvah". Or would it be the day my beloved brother Howard received his smicha, his ordination as an Orthodox rabbi. Perhaps it would be my wedding day, the moment my entire family stood under the chuppah while Howard officiated. It might even be the births of his grandchildren, the future generation of the Jewish people.

Nothing prepared Noah or me for my father's answer. As we stared blankly at each other, he raised his hand and pointed his index finger at us, and said with great conviction, "The proudest moments of my life vere vhen I killed Germans and Poles."

TWO

RSVP to a Funeral

The chain reaction of evil - hate begetting hate, wars producing more wars - must be broken, or else we shall be plunged into the dark abyss of annihilation.
- Martin Luther King, Jr.

Friday, July 30, 2010, just one day after my father died, the funeral director from Shalom Memorial Park Cemetery, a friend from my synagogue, came to my home to discuss the funeral arrangements. I planned a traditional burial in accordance with the Orthodox Jewish laws that my father had specified in his will.

In addition, I opted to hire a shomer, a guard who accompanies the body and recites T'Hilim (psalms) continuously until the burial. My father had not requested this added expense in his will, but I was comforted knowing that he was not left alone over the Sabbath.

The funeral director suggested that I post the information on Facebook, since I had decided not to place an obituary in the newspaper. At first it struck me as quite odd, but she handed me a printed postcard with details and directions on how to put the funeral information onto the site. When I went to Facebook, I posted the funeral information accidentally as an "event" instead of "what's on your mind". So it appeared as an invitation, and I began to receive RSVPs from my friends on Facebook.

Feeling very awkward about the posting, I decided not to engage in any further activity and completely ignored the site.

It wasn't until Saturday night at about 10:45 that I went online and noticed an inordinate number of suspicious and unrecognizable emails on my Facebook page. Logging onto the site, I discovered that the messages posted were from strangers and that I had inadvertently invited people from all over the world to my father's funeral. There were more than fifty unopened messages, and I began to read them one by one. A surge of terror quickly overtook my body, and I began to shake uncontrollably.

"Zigathon" wrote:

"Fucking Jews!"

"Adolf Hitler" wrote:

"Kann ich einige jüdische Leute mit ihm begraben? Ich habe zu viele Leichen." (Can I put more Jewish people in the ground? I have too many corpses.)

"Johny" wrote:

"Satan will be pleased, another bitch ass to fuck, say hello to Saddam from me."

"Andrey" wrote:

"5th of August Munting time"

"Sally" wrote:

"Rest in piss you dead FUCK."

"Muhammed Hashmilah'd" wrote:

"Allah never spares."

"Ima" wrote:

"Will there be cake? and fapping?"

Needless to say, these morbidly sick and anti-Semitic postings were too much for me to handle. I wanted them all to disappear from the site immediately.

"Noah," I asked helplessly, "can you remove all of these nasty responses from Facebook? Also, please delete the posted information regarding the funeral."

By 11:00 p.m., we had completely cleared the funeral information from my Facebook site. I was relieved and was not expecting any more tumult, but at 11:03 the house phone rang.

"Karen," a friend asked, "what's going on? Why did you cancel the funeral?"

Intensely frustrated, I said:

"The funeral is not canceled. My father is still dead. He hasn't risen up! Just be there tomorrow morning."

But emails kept pouring onto my site after that, with the repeated question, "Will there be a funeral tomorrow morning?"

I was restless all night, unable to get much sleep. Maybe I was the one, instead of my father, who should have had the shomer. As I was lying in bed, I thought about how fate had been cruel to my father. Prejudice and violence had been relentless in his life and had even followed him to his grave.

THREE

The Eulogy

Being unwanted, unloved, uncared for, forgotten by everybody,
I think that is a much greater hunger, a much greater poverty
than the person who has nothing to eat.
-Mother Teresa

My mother always looked forward to spending time with her grand-children. My brother Howard had one daughter, but his family lived in New Jersey; so I brought my son Max over as often as possible. When Max was a baby, my mother loved cradling him, giving him his bottle, and feeding him. Having her children and grandchildren well fed was very important to her. God forbid we should ever be hungry or without food, because my mother would be terribly upset. She overfed my brothers and me when we were young, and we all became fat. In the 1950s, a plump baby meant a healthy baby, and she embraced that philosophy. She was simply not concerned about our weight. Once she told me that she asked the pediatrician if we were adequately nourished; she was concerned because we kept a kosher household and thus our diet lacked bacon, ham, and shellfish.

When I was in grade school, my mother would pack oversized lunches. My sandwiches were always big, sloppy, and soggy; when I bit into one, the Miracle Whip and sandwich spread would drip all over my hands. As a volunteer at my school on "hot lunch" days, my mom always gave every student in line a double portion of food until she was told to stop.

As a teenager, I was extremely tall and very zaftig. I was described as "pleasingly plump"—something you might say about a raisin. I found it difficult to fit clothes to my body size, so my mom would often take me to a dressmaker to ensure clothes fit me perfectly. She would also take me to Devon Avenue, the main street in our neighborhood, to buy clothes at a shop called "Chubettes". Imagine the complete embarrassment I felt when I told my friends where I shopped.

Whenever she traveled to visit Howard during the holidays, she would bring him homemade gelfite fish and jars of her chicken, matzah ball, and kreplach soup on the plane with her.

After Max was born, she would babysit for me at a moment's notice. She would also often bring along an extra pot of my favorite beet or cabbage borsht and a sweet apple and cheese kugel for my family. As a toddler, Max would sit on her lap, and she would read to him for hours at a time. She had a stack of books and toys in her house just so he would enjoy going there to play.

In the pictures we have of my mother in her late teens and early twenties, she looks like a 1940s Hollywood movie star. Her features were perfectly symmetrical, and when she pulled her thick, dark-brown hair back off her face, you could see her big, beautiful brown eyes. When she smiled, she had the most beautifully shaped white teeth, and her eyes twinkled with innocence.

My mom and I talked on the phone every day, sometimes about absolutely nothing. She wanted to hear the tiniest details about her grandchildren. Her children and grandchildren brought her love and joy and were her focal point in life. She was also a worrier. If she didn't hear from my brothers or me by the end of each day, she would be alarmed. All she needed was a quick five-second phone call every evening to know that we were all safe, and then she could retire to bed.

Whenever my brothers and I traveled abroad, we knew we had to call her. In those days we had this secret code of communicating with her by phone, which I never liked doing because it was cheating the system. We would use public pay phones and call collect. We would dial the operator and say, "I want to make a collect call to 'Alice Fine'" (the Yiddish word "alles" means "all is"). The operator would then ask us for Alice's number, and we would give our home number. When the operator called my mother at home and asked if "Alice Fine" would like to accept the collect call, my mother refused the call. This worked out well in my family, because my father would not pay for these extraneous phone charges, and my mother could stop worrying—at least for that day.

When Howard was an assistant rabbi living in Baltimore, my mother called him one night and he did not answer the phone. After a few more unanswered calls and going sleepless all night, she did what I thought any mother would do; she called the Baltimore police. Early the next morning, my brother woke up to the doorbell ringing at his home and was astonished to find the police at his front door.

"Are you Howard Kaplan?" the police officers asked.

"Yes," my brother responded nervously. "What is going on here?"

"Your mother called us and is concerned about you," they said. "You didn't answer the phone last night. You better call her."

On a pleasant summer day, August 15, 1991, my mom and I returned to her condominium after an early afternoon of shopping together with Max, who was two and a half years old at that time. As I put Max down for an afternoon nap in her bed, the phone rang. I picked it up and it was my sister-in-law from New Jersey.

"Karen," she said, "I have some terrible news."

"What's going on?" I asked tentatively.

"Howard is dead," she said.

"What! What are you talking about? "I asked.

"Howard always wakes up very early in the morning. Today he didn't get up, and I let him sleep in. Finally, I went into the bedroom to check on him, and he wouldn't wake up. His body was already cold. I called for emergency help, but it was too late. They could not revive him. Will you tell your mother for me?"

In that moment my world froze. I gasped, and the receiver dropped to the floor as my hands covered my mouth. I did not want my mother to hear me. I don't believe this, I thought. None of this is making any sense.

Howard lived in Cliffside Park, New Jersey, with his wife and two young children. He was a pulpit rabbi for a small Orthodox congregation. My brother was thirty-five years old and in good health, a pillar of physical strength at over six-foot-six. He had no medical condition that had warned us of any kind of ill health, and he was in great physical condition. When I was a little girl, Howard would wrap his huge arms around me and hug me; he made me feel protected from the world. He had a big heart, and I felt loved by him.

How could he not wake up? This is impossible, I thought. My heart began pounding faster. Dear God, how do I tell my mother?

"Karen, what's the matter?" my mom asked as she walked into the room.

"Mommy, you need to sit down," I said.

A look of terror appeared on my mother's face. She knew something was God-awful wrong, so she sat down.

"Helene just called, and she told me Howard is dead," I cried.

My mother screamed and went into shock. From that day forward she was never quite the same. Every day she dwelt on the loss of her first-born child.

The next day, my husband drove me to a travel agency, and I dragged myself into the office while he waited in the car. Hunched over and grasping the sides of the desk, I forced myself to speak.

"Please," I said to the travel agent, "book five round-trip tickets to Newark Airport—for tomorrow. I am going to bury my brother."

We left Max with his other grandparents and waited for my brother Barry to fly to Chicago from California. Then we all flew to New Jersey. I could barely eat--or keep any food down when I did eat. I couldn't sleep. The energy was zapped out of my body, and I lost ten pounds. We were all in shock. We sat at the funeral in silence--like mannequins, barely moving. At the gravesite, my father began to recite the kaddish, the mourner's prayer. He started to tremble and wail, so I stood next to him and held his arm because I was afraid he was going to accidentally fall into the grave.

My one regret was that I was not able to write and deliver a eulogy for Howard. I was simply incapable at that time—nor was any member of my immediate family. The shock persisted for several days, and his death has overshadowed our lives as we have carried this deep sadness for many years. It has been twenty years since my brother died, and I still think about him all the time.

———◆———

Six years later, on August 7, 1997, within six weeks of her diagnosis of stage IV uterine cancer, my mother passed away at the age of sixty-two. Again I was too mentally distraught and physically weak to even consider writing a eulogy. Shock, anger, and despair once again pervaded every single fiber of my body. I was incapable of doing anything more than taking care of the physical needs of my three young children and myself.

———◆———

During my freshman year of high school in 1976, our family moved into this condominium in the West Rogers Park neighborhood, and I lived there for ten years—until I married. West Rogers Park is a Jewish neighborhood of Chicago where synagogues line every block of the main streets, along with kosher bakeries, butcher shops, delicatessens, and religious bookstores. A Jewish community center, senior center, nursing homes, and private Jewish schools are also all in the neighborhood.

I remembered a few happy occasions when I lived in this condo. My mother made me a sweet sixteen luncheon and invited my school friends and some close relatives to celebrate. We shopped at Marshall Field's department store in Skokie where I picked out a maroon velvet blazer, white turtle neck and a plaid skirt for my party. She cooked and baked all the food and served my favorite chocolate cake and chocolate chip mandelbread. My mother hired a high school student who drew caricatures for each of my guests. Other friends had their parties in hotels, but that didn't matter to me; my mother made me feel extra-special on that day.

For my mother's fiftieth birthday, in 1984, I surprised her with a party. Our relatives wondered why my father wasn't there and I didn't know; I was actually relieved he didn't show up. There always seemed to be tension when he was around and I worried incessantly what he might say or do in public since his temperament was mercurial.

Any emotional attachments that I had to this apartment had long disappeared. I had married in 1986 and moved to Deerfield, a northern suburb of Chicago. That is where we raised our three children: Max, Noah and Raquel.

By 2009, my mother had already been gone for twelve years, and there was no indication that she had ever lived there. My father had given me all of her photos and albums after her death, and I took her personal items that she would have wanted me to keep.

In November 2009, about nine months before my father died, Barry flew to Chicago to close on my father's condo, because my father made him co-owner. Barry dealt with the realtor and attorney and took control of selling the apartment. He likes to take charge of business matters, especially real estate, since he has been financially successful in this market. When it comes to business, Barry believes that he is smarter than most people, so he can become impatient and easily agitated. His temper can flare readily, and, like my father, he expresses his anger freely.

My father had been living in a nursing home for several months and that week was particularly difficult for Barry and me; we spent many hours each day physically cleaning up my father's place, which was full of a lifetime of his hoarded objects. In the kitchen there were warped wooden cabinets containing two sets of neatly stacked dishes—all of them chipped. My mother and father always maintained a kosher home, so we had one set of dairy dishes and one set of meat dishes. There were also cracked glasses, tarnished flatware, broken pots and pans, stale spices, and empty pickle jars with their separate lids. My father never threw anything out because he always believed that there was value in everything.

File cabinets were spread throughout the house—in the closets and in the corners of many rooms. They were filled with years of bank statements and outdated bills and receipts, along with all the necessary personal files on insurance, wills, and property information. Boxes of tax returns dating from the 1960s, packages of old mothballs, broken and antiquated household appliances, old-fashioned shopping carts, unusable luggage, small boxes filled with bent and rusted screws and nails, and more--all were carefully organized in the closets around the house. My job was to rummage through all the papers and clothes, while my brother worked on clearing away the heavier items.

Barry began in the bedroom and unlocked our father's desk drawer. He was astonished to find his own bar-mitzvah watch, silver and gold jewelry, and his coin collection all neatly arranged inside. All these years Barry had thought that he had lost these valuable personal items when we moved from our old apartment in East Rogers Park to this condo in 1976.

Shocked at his discovery, Barry shouted, "Come here, Karen, and look what Daddy has been hiding all these years. Can you believe this? He took all my bar mitzvah checks and cash at the time of my bar mitzvah, but I never thought he would steal my personal belongings. He is a ganef (thief). He is rotten and a low life! I hate him!"

I looked at all the contents in the drawer and said, "I can't believe he stole that from you," but then I realized I could believe it. "I'm sure we'll find more things as we continue to clean up."

Barry left the room, and I stayed in my father's bedroom to clear out his closets and drawers. I found brightly colored plaid pants and polyester suits, along with dozens of old buttoned-down shirts. I noticed a sky-blue polyester suit that I recall him wearing back in the early 1970s. Shoes with worn-out soles were stacked in the shoe racks on the floor of the closet, plus an old tie rack that held ties from decades long gone.

As I noticed my father's old and cracked leather belts hanging in his closet, my mind flashed back to him taking his belt and whipping my brothers when they were young. Those memories had faded away, and I had not thought about them for many years. As a little girl, I was terrified when I saw my brothers being beaten by my father. I would run and hide in the closet of my room, covering my ears to drown out their screams.

On the top shelf of his closet, he had carefully stacked papers, labeled boxes of checkbooks from various banks, along with office supplies. There were used and new paperclips, boxes of staples, and a diverse array of rubber bands--all organized into plastic baggies. As I was removing these items from the top shelf, I found a large manila envelope that was tucked and concealed under another box up in the top corner. It was stuffed with papers. When I opened the envelope, I saw pages with detailed lists of women, their addresses, and what seemed to be number codes for entry into their apartments. There were also old photos of my father with many different women. Then I found dozens of love letters dated throughout the course of my parents' marriage. There was even a picture of him and his girlfriend, Beba, the woman he lived with at the time of his death, standing together in a hotel lounge. The photo indicated that it had been taken in 1995, two years before my mother died. I sat down on my father's bed staring at all the pictures and attempting to read some letters—but I couldn't read them. My hands were trembling, and I felt my stomach drop. I was sickened by my discovery.

I was unable to utter a sound or move an inch. Did my mother ever suspect my father of having affairs? How dare he betray her! How could he do this to our family!

When we were young, he forced us to observe all the Jewish rituals and traditions. He chose to send us to religious day school so that we could study the Torah, the Jewish laws, and the history of our people. He instilled all of these Jewish traditions and values in us while his own behavior was morally reprehensible. He was not only a thief, but also an adulterer. What a hypocrite! I thought. For a long while I sat there in silence with these thoughts churning in my mind.

Finally, Barry walked back into the room, wondering why I was so quiet. He noticed the letters covering the bedspread. I quickly snapped out of my daze when Barry picked up one of the letters to read. His face became flushed and turned bright red. He bashed his fists on the furniture, screamed at the top of his lungs, sobbed out loud, and yelled, "This man does not deserve a eulogy for what he has done to our family!"

I sat there thinking, maybe, just maybe, I could read one of these love letters at his funeral, when it happens. But then I shuddered at the mere thought of exposing this particular family secret to my family and friends.

During the next eight months, my father's physical health deteriorated, and his dementia progressed at a rapid pace. As he became considerably weaker, I really began to think about writing his eulogy. What would I say? I tried to remember loving moments, but only one came to mind. How would I write a respectable eulogy for my father that would also be truthful?

My father died on Thursday, July 29, 2010, in the early morning, just a half hour before I arrived at the hospice center with my cousin, Alisha. How I wished he had chosen a life filled with love instead of hate. How I wished he had treated my mother and my siblings with care and respect. I longed for a loving relationship with my father. I longed for him to hold me and hug me, and I wanted to hear him say to me, just once in my life, "I love you." He chose not to.

At the hospice center I met the Orthodox rabbi, who seemed genuinely concerned. He was a tall, extra-large man with a huge stomach. His face was aged, and his hair and short beard were all white. He wore a simple black suit, white shirt, a black kippah, and white tzitzit (knotted ritual fringes) protruding from his sides. He had a pleasant disposition and appeared very humble and kind. I asked him if he would officiate at my father's funeral, and he agreed. He wanted to know some personal details of my father's life so that he could speak a few words on his behalf at the funeral.

"What did your father do for a living?" he asked.

"When he first immigrated to America," I said, "he taught at Hebrew school and became a shammas (a caretaker in the synagogue). Eventually, he became a social worker. Throughout his life he was a Baal Koreh (a Torah reader) for Shabbat services at several synagogues--until he could no longer walk to synagogue."

"Ah, very nice. He was a religious man and a mensch!" exclaimed the rabbi.

I responded immediately, but politely, "Rabbi, being a religious man does not necessarily imply that he was a mensch. The one trait does not necessarily equate with the other. But I would be honored if you would perform all the rituals and prayers at my father's funeral in an Orthodox manner, as he requested in his will. I want to abide by his wishes. And I will deliver the eulogy."

Within minutes, I called my brother, Barry, in California to notify him of my arrangements, mentioning that the Orthodox rabbi at the hospice care center would officiate at our father's funeral.

"I don't want him to exaggerate Daddy's personal character and speak lies. I will not sit through a fake funeral. And I don't want a eulogy to be read," Barry commanded. "He doesn't deserve one."

"Not to worry," I said, "I already spoke to the rabbi and discussed the arrangements with him. I will have prepared a eulogy, and only the truth will be spoken."

My father's funeral was held on Sunday morning, August 1, 2010. After the rabbi recited the Twenty-third Psalm, one of the traditional prayers read at the funeral, my oldest son, twenty-one-year-old Max, spoke articulately on behalf of all my children and gave a brief, appropriate, and insightful eulogy to his grandfather.

Then I approached the podium. I was carrying a folder with six neatly typed sheets of paper, and my hands were trembling. A synopsis of my father's life was about to be revealed to my extended family and friends, and I was unsure how everyone would react. Standing at the podium, I peered out at my captive audience, took a deep breath, and began to deliver a eulogy to my father.

My Father's Eulogy

God doesn't give you the people you want. God gives you the people you need--to help you, to hurt you, to love you, to leave you, and to make you into the person you were meant to be.

My father, Avrum Jankel Szteinsapir, was born on May 21, 1921, and grew up with his family on a duck farm in the village of Rajgród (pronounced "Rye grod"), Poland, roughly forty five miles northwest of Bialystok. His father, Chaim Shlomo, died in January 1927 at the age of fifty-two from a stomach ailment-- when my dad was only six years old. His mother, Beila, who was born in Jenova, Poland, had married Chaim Shlomo in 1913 in Rajgród. When her husband died, she was left to tend to the family farm and home with my father and the rest of her children.

Gitel (Tova), my father's eldest sibling, moved to Bialystok in 1927, and then moved to Lodz from 1933 until 1939 preparing on Hachsharah (a training program for Jews who wished to settle in Palestine). Tova was a chalutzah, part of the Zionist pioneer movement, and went to settle in Palestine (long before there was a state of Israel). Avrum's other siblings included Chaya Esther, Leah, (married with a baby) and Josephine, nicknamed Yoshpe. The youngest child was Yehuda Leizer, Avrum's younger brother, who died when he was two years old. I was named after

Chaya Esther and Leah, the two older sisters, both of whom died in the Holocaust.

As a young boy, my father went to cheder to study Torah, the Talmud, Jewish law, and history. He learned Hebrew in school, spoke Yiddish and Polish at home, and was also fluent in Russian and German. Later in life, when he came to the United States, he learned English and Spanish. His Spanish pronunciations sounded a bit odd since he always spoke Spanish with his Polish accent. Other than being in Hebrew school, he spent the rest of his time working on the family farm. Extra help was needed to operate and manage the farm, so my grandmother, Beila, hired two Ukrainian workers.

Life was becoming increasingly violent for the Jews in Poland in the 1930s. Pogroms and riots against the Jews broke out in the bigger cities, and often the violence spiraled into the nearby smaller villages. World War II began when the Germans invaded Poland on September 1st, 1939. On June 22, 1941, several townspeople of Rajgród, headed by the two Ukrainian workers my grandmother had hired, came to murder my father's family. When my son Noah interviewed my father a few years ago, about his life in Poland, my father described how he witnessed the death of his mother, and two of his sisters, he broke down and wept, something I saw him do only twice in my life. As he recalled this gruesome story, he described how his mother, Beila, pleaded with the murderers to kill her quickly. But they were without a shred of mercy, forcing her to suffer a long and drawn-out death. Yoshpe, Leah and her family were also tortured and brutally murdered by the mob. My father managed to hide as he witnessed this unimaginable horror, but he witnessed it from his hiding place.

Eventually, my father learned that Chaya Esther had died in 1942 when she was sent to Treblinka. Tova, the one sibling who immigrated to Palestine, was the only survivor from his entire family. With no one else alive in his household, he was forced to flee into the forests of Eastern Europe, where he lived during the war years. Food was always scarce, and living conditions in the forest were deplorable. He had to kill Germans and Poles to survive. He would always remind me not to complain about the bitter cold weather during winters in Chicago. He was forced to survive the brutal winters in the forests of Poland sleeping outside on a bed of snow. At one point during those treacherous years, he was taken in by a family from Hamburg, Germany, who hid him for a while from the Nazis. They fed him and clothed him and took care of his physical needs.

During this period, he found a Polish passport and used it for identification. The passport had the identity of a younger man whose name was Aryeh Kaplan. So by assuming this identity, he was able to pass himself off as too young to be sent off to fight on the Russian front. His life was spared and so he decided to retain the Arie Kaplan identity; in fact he continued to use that name throughout his life.

World War II ended in May 1945, but not before almost three and a half million Polish Jews, the largest Jewish community of Europe, had been murdered. My father was unsure of where to begin a new life. He knew that malaria was rampant in Palestine and another impending war against the Jews was almost certain. So my father left Germany, along with hundreds of thousands of other European emigrants, and immigrated into the United States, settling in Chicago in 1951. He met my beloved mother, Harriet Kaplan, (may God continue to bless her soul), at a Jewish Dance on the west side of Chicago. They married in 1954 and had three children. My oldest brother, Howard, (may God rest his soul) was born in 1956, Barry was born in 1958 and I was born in 1962.

Once settled in Chicago, my father studied at the College of Jewish Studies and received a Hebrew teaching certificate in 1952. My father worked for synagogues, reading Torah and teaching Hebrew school throughout his lifetime. He continued to read Torah well into his early eighties--until he could no longer walk to synagogue. He attended Roosevelt University and received a Bachelors of Art degree in 1955. In 1968 he became a certified social worker for the State of Illinois, where he spent much of his time allocating welfare funds to the poor. He was also involved with a Holocaust organization trying to raise money to build a monument in Chicago in memory of the six million Jews that perished in the war.

When we were very young, we moved to the Rogers Park neighborhood in Chicago because my father wanted to raise his family in a Jewish neighborhood where we could walk to synagogue to attend holiday and Shabbat services. We all attended public school for a while, but he decided that, after his sons were coming home from public school singing

Christmas carols, he would send his three children to private Orthodox Day school for elementary and secondary education.

In August 1991, my beloved brother, Rabbi Howard Kaplan, was found dead in his apartment in Cliffside Park, NJ, where he resided with his wife and two young children Judith and Michael (three years and eight months old respectively). My father shed tears as he recited the Kaddish at Howard's grave site.

In August 1997, my beloved mother, Harriet Kaplan, passed away from uterine cancer. So my dad spent his remaining years living with Beba Landau in the uptown area of Chicago, where she tirelessly helped care for my father, especially during these last few years of his life.

These final couple of weeks of my father's life were filled with intense pain and suffering. It was a long and drawn out death. The doctors and the staff in the ICU were shocked to see him live well beyond their expectation, to see him fight to survive to the bitter end. But he was accustomed to this way of living.

My dad and his family were victims of torture and persecution; in a way it was a trademark of my family heritage. My father spent years tracing his family ancestry, and he discovered that we come from a direct lineage of Rabbis dating back to the Spanish Inquisition. In the late 1400s, Spanish Jews who refused to convert to Christianity were expelled from their country. Many migrated east and eventually, after many generations, ended up in Eastern Europe. Suffering has always seemed to follow the Jews of Europe throughout these last five hundred years; generation upon generation of torture and murder. Generations of fear plagued my family and my people. This energetic imprint of terror and mass killings has permeated the lifeline of my family's and my culture's fabric of life.

I was born into a family that carried the negative energy of fear and darkness. I am also of the first generation of Jews born out of the Holocaust. I have identified myself as a child of a survivor, and I have felt an extremely heavy burden placed on me; the burden of ensuring that I continue to keep the Jewish people alive and keep alive the horrific memories of the Holocaust that have been part of my family and people.

"We will not let Hitler win, nor allow any other anti-Semite to exterminate our people! Never again! We must follow the ancient laws and observances of our people so that we can continue to flourish and repopulate the lost six million. We must never forget how the world treated us. We must survive!"

These were the predominant thoughts and themes during my childhood in my household, and the same ideology was reinforced in my private Hebrew day school education. This fear of of extermination and struggle for survival have passed in my family from generation to generation--like cellular DNA. This fear of eradication permeated my daily existence; it is a fear that children of Holocaust survivors always understand and feel.

Living life with a Holocaust survivor in my family was intense and difficult. My father was burdened with this fear and bitterness throughout his life. He hardened his heart and vowed to never let go of that pain. He never left those gruesome years in Poland behind, and he and my family suffered immensely for it. The fear conquered his mind, body, and spirit. He lived life as if he were still running in the forests like a frightened animal hunted by its predator. This veil was cast over our family. I carried this fear as if I were expecting someone lurking in the background, waiting to seize me so that I could be the next victim of violence, just like the Jews who were rounded up and taken to the slaughterhouses of Europe.

My dad was filled with rage, hatred, and revenge against the whole world. He endured too much pain in his lifetime, a life that no one should ever have to experience. So his life experiences tainted his soul. I recognize that carrying this fear has not served me, protected me, or benefited me in any way—certainly not healed me. It pollutes my mind, body, and spirit, leaving me to live with fear, bitterness, and sadness for my family and my people.

But now I am taking a new pathway to make healthy changes for myself, my family, and our future generations. I am healing from all this bitterness and lifting the veil of these thought forms that haunt us. These family memories do not need to control me anymore. I only wish that my father would have learned to forgive the people of his past so that he could have healed from all the trauma in his lifetime.

I believe that life is meant to be lived fully, filled with compassion, peace, joy, forgiveness, and especially love. This was a concept that was unattainable for my father. In a way, my father, his family, and all the prior generations sacrificed themselves to being victims of hatred and violence so that I can benefit from understanding the true gift of life, so that I can learn the true lessons and purpose of my life and appreciate life to the fullest. Therefore, I am deeply indebted to my father, his family, and all my ancestors for sacrificing their lives over these past five hundred years.

To my father, Arie, as your neshamah (soul) leaves this earth plane and travels to the ethereal plane, as your soul frees itself from the constraints of this physical world, I pray that God speeds the healing of your soul. I pray that all the fear, anger, and bitterness that have cast a shadow of darkness on your soul be lifted so that you can move forward with peace, joy, and love.

Yevarechecha adonai veyishmerecha.
May God bless you and protect you.

Ya'er adonai panav elecha veyichunecha.
May God's face give light to you and be gracious to you.

Yisa adonai panav elecha veyasem lecha shalom.
May God's face be lifted toward you and bestow upon you peace.

Remember, God doesn't give us the people we want; God gives us the people we need--to help us, to hurt us, to leave us, to love us, and to make us into the people we were meant to be.

When I finished delivering the eulogy, the room seemed strangely silent. As I surveyed the funeral hall, I saw some of my friends wiping the tears from their eyes. The rabbi looked stunned as he stared at me, speechless. My children stood, reached out their arms, and hugged me as I returned to my seat. My brother sat there bewildered. He stared at me and seemed to be lost in thought. For a brief moment it seemed that the lifetime of hatred he carried against my father had dissipated from his body. He sat back more relaxed in his chair and seemed stupefied by the powerful message I had delivered in that eulogy. A tremendous sense of relief came over me as we waited for the rabbi to continue the service. I knew that at this juncture of my life, I was determined to continue this path of healing. I believe this was one of the proudest moments in my life.

FOUR

Money

━━━

"Hath not a Jew eyes? Hath not a Jew hands, organs, dimensions, senses, affections, passions; fed with the same food, hurt with the same weapons, subject to the same diseases, heal'd by the same means, warm'd and cool'd by the same winter and summer, as a Christian is? If you prick us, do we not bleed? If you tickle us, do we not laugh? If you poison us, do we not die? And if you wrong us, do we not revenge? If we are like you in the rest, we will resemble you in that.
-Shylock in *The Merchant of Venice* Act 3, Scene 1

I was weaned on my father's hatred, and feared that I would turn out like him but had never met or read about anyone like him, until I read *The Merchant of Venice* in high school. I remember sweating as we read about this Jewish man who is ridiculed and humiliated by those who still seek to borrow money from him. My father similarly felt driven to take revenge, but instead of asking for just one pound of flesh, felt completely justified in taking out his anger on the entire world.

One day I was paying bills at my kitchen table, and I heard a loud noise from outside. I looked out the window and saw a gray and white squirrel brazenly staring at me and hissing with his little paws swiping at me as he jumped onto the windowsill. I thought he was trying to tell me something, and we stared at each other for a couple of minutes. My friends laugh that these things always seem to happen to me, but I swear I thought I saw the face of my father on that squirrel.

After minutes had passed, I said to the squirrel (he couldn't hear me because I was inside, thankfully), "if you have something to say then say it!" I got up and hurried out of the room. The next day a crab apple was left on that same windowsill, in the exact place where the squirrel was standing. I might have been mistaken, but I was sure that the squirrel had left it there for me. Who leaves crab apples on my windowsill? I think the message was that I should stop worrying, that I would always have food and would always be able to feed my children.

I started thinking about squirrels, and how they're so resourceful as they instinctively and wisely prepare for the winter. Uncertain if food will be abundant in the coming months, they actively search, collect and bury all sorts of berries, nuts, acorns, roots and seeds.

My father behaved similarly. He used to spend all day carefully squirreling things away to protect himself against possible future calamities. One of my favorite cousins is Jerry, a brilliant member of Mensa, yet very sociable. Over the years, our families have celebrated all the Jewish holidays together. Cousin Jerry helped me understand the relationship my father had with money during his marriage. When my father's health was declining, I was thinking about my mother and wondering about my parents' early life together, and I knew that Jerry would be able to talk honestly about the past.

Jerry is a gregarious, highly energetic man who commands attention. He is filled with amusing stories from his childhood and has a flair for sharing them. At sixty-three years old, six feet tall with a stocky build, Jerry always greets everyone with a huge, warm and friendly hug. He's a mensch, the kind of guy who always gives everyone the benefit of the doubt.

As another child of Holocaust survivors, Jerry is cognizant of survivor's idiosyncrasies and quite understanding of their post-war-like mentality. He is a Vietnam vet and has a great deal of tolerance for people who have been through wars.

My Grandpa Max and Jerry's grandfather were brothers and both families were very close. Sarah, (Jerry's mother) and my Bubbie Rae were the best of friends, so Jerry spent a lot of time as a child in my grandparents' home. According to Jerry, my mother was never around when he came by to visit with his family. He was thirteen years younger, so he often played with my mother's younger brother Albert. But as an adult, he liked my mother and they reminisced about their families. My father would speak to Jerry infrequently but when they talked, the topic revolved around World War II and Judaism.

"Your father's most prominent characteristic that was unanimously agreed upon by both of our families was his cheapness. They nicknamed him karger (cheapskate)," exclaimed Jerry, who then told the first of many stories.

Jerry recalled that once at a cousin's club, in front of the relatives, my father declared, "my wife, Harriet does not need to buy a new dress, she has her old ones and can wear them until they become schmattes (rags). Then she can give me the old ones and I'll buy replacements."

"I thought your mother's cousin, Bella Kazen, was going to rip your father's tongue out of his mouth back then," chuckled Jerry.

He understood my father's war-like mentality and recalled my father's description of how he survived in the forests.

"The conditions in the forest were extreme," said Jerry. "Your father had nothing but the soiled, lice-infested clothes on his back. His body was overrun with these tiny parasites and at night he would take off his clothes, shake them over the fire and listen to them crackle to death," commented Jerry. "If he needed some new clothes, he would remove them from a dead body. He thought that clothes were just meant to keep him covered and warm during those awful winters."

(My father always took pride in his appearance but he would not spend money. He expected my mother to launder and iron his shirts and his pants, at his request on a moment's notice. Once a month he would sit on the back porch of our apartment shining his shoes with thick black muddy polish and a schmatte. His shoes were old but he buffed them to delay having to buy new ones, as he did with everything. He would never leave the house without shaving and he carried a small black comb in his pant's pocket to insure that his hair was always combed back neatly off his face. I would often see him staring at himself in the mirror at home and in the car rear view mirror to insure that his hair was perfectly in place.)

"We sent out my bar mitzvah invitations and never received a response from your family," recalled Jerry, "I suspect that your dad removed the stamp from the response envelope and used it for himself."

(Jerry was right. When I was young, my father would inspect the household mail to see if the stamps had been dated and marked by the post office. If not then he would gingerly remove them from the envelopes before handing us our mail.)

Jerry vividly remembers when my dad approached him at his bar mitzvah party and handed him a ball-point pen; everyone noticed that it was a free gift from a bank. "At that point, my mother and your bubbie were so angry with him for all his meshugaas (craziness) they avoided him and never spoke to his face again," exclaimed Jerry.

(My father didn't care; he didn't like anyone and hardly anyone liked him. Growing up, he had nicknames for everyone. Only now I realize they weren't sweet or endearing; they were derogatory. He meant to degrade and belittle. Such behavior made him feel better about himself. He called my bubbie "The Alteh Machasheifa" (old witch) since he referred to my mother as "Machasheifa" (witch). He was amused and use to smirk when he also called my mother "Meiskeit" (ugly thing). My Grandpa Max was named the "Alteh Chazir" (old pig) while Jerry's mother was nick- named "Meshuganah" (crazy one). One of our relatives who had a huge nose was referred as the "Langeh neiz" (long nose). Our next-door neighbor had a glass eye and when my father fought with him he called him the "Blinder Ferd" (blind horse). My mother was good friends with a family down our street and he called the husband "Farfoylt Moyl" (stinking, decayed mouth) while his wife was the "Greena Cousina" a derogatory term for Eastern European immigrants. My brothers and I did not escape from the barrage of insults. Howard was called the "Nar" or fool, Barry was "The No Goodnik" and I had a generic name of "The Maydl" or the girl. Even the Asian bank tellers had nicknames. He advised us to stay away from them since they wouldn't cave in to his constant demands for attention and deals. He called them the "Kleiner Eigen" (small eyes). He also had a habit of calling women "Kurvas" (prostitutes).)

Jerry continued the interview with a story from earlier in my parent's marriage. He recalls walking in their apartment and noticing a large, dangerous gaping hole in the kitchen floor. Jerry asked my dad if he was going to repair it and my father replied, "There is no need, just walk around it."

Jerry then remembered the time that my father put a significant amount of savings into an uptown bank that soon went bankrupt. Everyone in the family was tickled pink, and said "Azey geschmacht" which meant they were glad he got screwed.

"Your bubbie figured that your mother was never going to see the money so they were happy to pieces that he lost it all. Eventually, his money was refunded," he commented with a smile.

At the end of the interview, Jerry said, "There was a raw spot between Arie and most people. His frugality made him despised among everyone who knew him. His cheapness tainted everything in his life. He was a bit extreme and some people just thought he was crazy. War had warped his perspective on life and he never adjusted to the prosperity in America."

Talking to my older cousin reminded me that while we were growing up, we had to be careful not to waste food, paper or anything that had potential value. My father would often rummage through the garbage cans to insure that nothing valuable was tossed out; sometimes he would take the spoiled food that my mother threw away and put it back into the refrigerator. We all had to be extremely cautious when opening gifts to avoid tearing the wrapping paper and bows since he would collect it all to reuse. At night he would follow us from room to room turning off the lights. In the car, he always waited until everyone was inside and then he would start the engine, even in the bitter cold. I thought all of this was normal, after all, I knew many survivors who behaved frugally; they would eat the crumbs that fell on the floor, take the extra bread, sugar, salt and jelly packets from the restaurant table before they left. My father seemed to have been years ahead of his time. Today, my daughter often says to me when I am not vigilant about recycling in my home, "Reduce, reuse and then recycle."

But, when my brothers and I were sick he refused to allow any medical attention. He simply was not going to pay the bill. To this day, my brother Barry blames him for not allowing any of us to seek medical attention, even in emergencies. Barry was ill for ten days at age 17 and my mother, against my father's command, finally took him to the doctor. By then the bacterial pneumonia had damaged his lungs. Today Barry is susceptible to lung infections and cannot tolerate the harsh Chicago winters, so he can only visit for short periods during mild seasons.

When we were young, my mother was deeply concerned that Howard was not physically maturing at a pace like other thirteen year old boys and took him to the pediatrician. The doctor suggested that Howard take growth hormone shots. My mother figured that since Barry was showing similar early signs of delayed onset puberty, she could have him treated during the same visit to prevent extra charges from the pediatrician's office (she learned that she must do everything to save few bucks and prevent additional fighting with my father). So Barry was inoculated with growth hormones at an age that was inappropriate for him. Suffice it to say that Barry's life was scarred physically, emotionally and psychologically from the trauma of these hormones; he was prevented from having a family.

From the time my mom died, my father's cheapness became more pronounced. During the intense hot and humid summers, he never put on the air conditioner and in the winter when I walked into his apartment, I could see my breath. He placed sofa cushions against the windows to keep the cold out and rarely put on the heat. He purchased the overly ripened and practically spoiled produce at the supermarket and always the day-old breads in the bakeries. He would frequent the Ark, a Jewish agency for the poor, to receive free meals, even though he could have bought the building and funded the program.

(To make up for his behavior, when he died, The Ark was the first charity to which I donated money.)

His neighbors in the condominium building always fought with him in the wintertime. They were afraid the pipes would freeze and burst because he would shut off the heat from his unit when he would leave to stay with his girlfriend, Beba. As the temperatures would drop below zero, he would call and expect me to drive twenty-five miles into the city to turn on his heat for that day. Then I was expected to return the following day and turn off the heat (but I never did).

Beba lived in a federally funded, high rise building for the poor in Uptown, a transient and high crime neighborhood of Chicago. Her native tongue was Russian and her English speaking skills were "so-so".

My father spoke to her in Yiddish and she replied in Russian. She was a seventy-five year old, red-headed widow with a pleasant disposition. She cared very deeply for my father and always attended to his needs. At first my father would just spend the weekends with her and would return back to his condominium during the week. After a few years he stayed with Beba all the time; she cooked for him and washed his clothes by hand, saving him lots of money. Once in a while, my father would bring over a kosher chicken. She would cook it for him, but he wouldn't even let her taste it. Beba asked him to pitch in for living expenses and so my father gave her $50.00 a month. Each year she requested more money and my father started getting upset with her.

"Vat should I do?" he asked me. "She vants more money from me. She is taking advantage of the situation."

"Daddy," I said, "you are basically living there for free. She takes care of you. You eat her food. You should pay her ten times the amount you are giving her. You can afford it. You are the one taking advantage of her." He was afraid she wouldn't let him live there, so my father unhappily gave her an additional $50.00 more each month.

On occasion, Barry and I would bring groceries to Beba's, and we'd try to sneak them into the apartment past my father. He always caught us and would complain bitterly, asking us instead to leave the food at his condo so he wouldn't have to share it with her. He was particularly upset if the bag contained salami because of his special fondness for cured meat. My father lived his life as if he never left the forest. Even though he didn't need to bear the frigid winters and the hot summers by eating worms, insects, berries and road kill and drinking the muddy waters to quench his thirst, he did the next best thing; he acted as if it was still necessary.

Realizing that it was becoming more and more difficult to manage his mail, bills and finances, my father had no choice but to give me the responsibility since Barry was not flying in from California to help much anymore (for years Barry would religiously come in every three months or so and spend time helping out my father). Each week, when I picked my father up from Beba's apartment, we went to his condo to collect the mail. He had a lot of incoming checks and dividends that needed to be deposited into his bank accounts. He would suspiciously watch me as I slowly opened every envelope and package and record the information into his books. He warned me over and over not to steal his money. I was so dutiful that I just reminded him over and over that I would never steal from my own father. And he never believed me because he thought that everyone lies and steals just like he did.

The first physical proof I saw of his nature was when I noticed that his insurance papers, driver's license and bank documents listed three different years of birth. I didn't understand and asked what year he was actually born. He said 1921 but he used 1916 to obtain early Medicare coverage. Then I realized why his girlfriend insisted that he was born in 1925. Beba was considerably younger than him and he lied to her about his age, as he did with my mother.

Jerry had explained that many of our relatives had commonly changed their names, ages and birth dates upon entering this country. Documentation in Europe was nonexistent and so many immigrants' names and birth dates were created at the time of entry into the country. "It was the norm, nothing unusual" said Jerry, "I had my last name changed three times."

"Yes, Jerry," I replied, "my father changed his last name to save his life. But my father lied about his year of birth only to save money." I was humiliated when I had to deal with government agencies, insurance companies and banks and publicly acknowledge that my father was a liar.

Jerry's interview solidified my realization that my father was a liar, cheater and a cheapskate from the very beginning of his marriage, if not well before. Everyone in the family seemed to have understood his character, but I was a grown adult before I really accepted it. There were so many letters in that stash I found when Barry and I cleaned out our father's condo while he was in the nursing home. This is from one particular mistress who candidly expressed his frugality. It was over twenty-five years since their affair when my father initiated contact and visited her in California. This is a segment of a letter she wrote to him after his short visit with her at her home on the west coast.

Arie:

I wasn't sure if I was going to write you ever again, but now that I'm over being angry with you for your cheap behavior, there are a few things I want to say to you. Since you can't hear me, either in person or by phone, I'm putting my thoughts in writing so you can rehash them.

Well, your fifteen hour visit with me is now history. I know you were happy with such a short visit. You planned it that way so it wouldn't cost you one cent, and in reflection, I see that's the only reason why you didn't stay with me. You were afraid that if you stayed with me during the day, it might cost you lunch and dinner. What a karger you are. Ethel K. had your number years ago, cheap, cheap, cheap. Never mind the fact that you were married.

You haven't changed either over the years; you are cheaper and tighter now than you ever were. I was thinking that as you aged and your children were grown and out of the house, you would let yourself enjoy some of the money and spend a few cents for a good time. But old habits die hard and what is ingrained stays. I now recall how you and your family left the motel in Los Angeles without paying. And how you left another motel in the middle of the night without paying, saying you were a man of the cloth and didn't conduct business on the Sabbath.

I must tell you what has bothered me about your visit. Here you were in my home with thousands of dollars worth of jewelry in my home with silver, crystal and china. No, you didn't see it but it was there. You kept counting and hiding your money. You pulled it out from your underwear; you kept checking your glass case. Your actions were so strange, they didn't go unnoticed.

What were you afraid of? That I was going to steal your money while you were a guest in my home? Paranoid, paranoid, paranoid. Your behavior was very obvious because it was strange, but because you were a guest in my home, I said nothing. I didn't want to spoil your time with me, but that hurt me. In fact, I recall in Chicago you would always leave your wallet under the car seat when we went out. Like I said, you haven't changed. Obviously you purposely planned just to say hello to me and not spend any time with me because your suitcase didn't even have a change of underwear or clothes. I don't know why you bothered with a suitcase at all. You see, your plans of circumventing spending a penny come to light in the end. Speaking of money, yes, I did lose a day's pay, and for your short visit and bad behavior, it wasn't worth it to me. So I lost money and you remained whole. That should make you feel good.

I was very distressed to learn that you didn't think to take your hearing aid to Los Angeles. Don't you think you would like to hear what people are saying to you, or doesn't it matter what other people say? Or were you saving wear and tear on your battery so you wouldn't have to buy a new battery eventually. As I told you, once you can't communicate with a person, the show is over. I knew you had a hearing problem for the past three years, you told me that during our telephone conversations, but you said you had a hearing aid, so I thought nothing more about it and was hoping that we would have lots of stories to tell one another. But when you have to put your ear next to my mouth and I have to shout because you left the aid, there is no joy in any storytelling.

Arie, I must tell you that no matter how much money you hoard away, you will never be a mensch. Here we didn't see each other for a good 25 years, and you didn't even have the decency to shave so that you look like a mensch. And like I told you over the phone before you left for California, a decent person doesn't come into someone's house for the first time empty handed (especially intending to be a house guest). Maybe that is the way you were raised but even in my broken home background, I was taught to be a mensch.

Well, I hope the plans you made with me for Poland materialize. Your prior letters and telephone conversations for the past 18 months led me to believe that we would make plans in person for such a trip. I actually had my homework all planned for such a trip. But with your 15 hour visit, half the time sleeping and the other half the time checking your money, there was no time for Poland planning. In the end: no plans, no Poland with me. I even doubt that you will spend the money on yourself to make such a trip.

Money is not my God, enjoying a decent lifestyle with pleasant friends is my aim in life. It's hard to find the friends; I thought you were one but I guess I was wrong, because friends care about each other and want to be with each other, regardless of gender. And, yes, friends do spend a buck on a friend, a meal never broke anyone.

God forbid anyone should ever have to depend on you for their sustenance. You would sooner see them croak.

Everything my father said and did revolved around his money; his extreme and radical relationship with money seemed justifiable in his mind. Controlling his money was one of the many ways he coped in life. During the Holocaust, some Jews survived by bribing officials; my father was never going to be at the mercy of anyone again and to insure his survivability he saved every dime, nickel and penny.

My father passed along his fear of surviving to all three of his children.

He wanted my brothers to be professionals and wanted me to marry an Orthodox man who could support a serious Jewish family lifestyle. Private Hebrew day school tuition was expensive. Kindergarten cost more than one year of my husband's medical school tuition. There would be thirteen years of schooling for all my children along with Jewish summer day and overnight camps, synagogue memberships, youth group memberships, trips to Israel and, of course, bar and bat mitzvoth celebrations. Huge amounts of money would be needed to create a Jewish environment insuring that they remain educated, devoted and unassimilated Jews.

My mother wanted me to marry a professional, preferably a Jewish doctor so that I could have a secure and prosperous life in the suburbs. She was a first-generation American, since her mother and father fled their homelands of Belarus and Lithuania from the pogroms and religious intolerance in the early 1900s. My mom's childhood was additionally scarred by the devastating effects of our country's great depression in the 1930s. So when I announced my engagement to a medical student, it was no surprise to my family and friends; they expected nothing less from me.

While writing this chapter, I experienced a powerful nightmare which forced me to feel the intensity of my father's fear of extermination.

In my nightmare, it is the early morning and my children and I are sleeping soundly upstairs in our bedrooms. My bedroom door is wide open and the house is dark and quiet. Suddenly a rustling noise comes from downstairs, jostles my sleep and I awake. The front doorknob turns and my heart started pounding. I clenched my sheets and my body freezes as I listen to someone breaking into my home. I lay in bed motionless, deciphering if my imagination was creating this possible scenario or if indeed this is truly happening. As the front door creaks open, I pray the stranger stays downstairs. Closely listening to every sound and movement, the noises begin to emanate from the staircase and become increasingly louder as the stranger climbs upstairs. Paralyzed with fright, I lay there numb and unable to move. Expecting the worst possible outcome for my children and me, I pray and say, "Dear God, please help me and protect my family."

Within moments the silhouette of a man stands in my bedroom doorway. He enters my room. My heart feels like it was going to jump out of my chest. He stands above my bed, stares at me and then crawls under my blankets quietly resting next to me. Terrified, I feel a pen near my hand and I quickly grab it and jab it directly into his heart. I kill him. Then I look at him and recognize him.

I woke up from this nightmare traumatized and crying, recalling my father's horror the day he witnessed his family murdered. In those horrid moments of my father's life, everything he loved and owned was viciously taken from him. He was forced to flee his home, running deliriously through the forests shell shocked. His trauma was so excruciating, that he forcibly tucked it away deep inside, never wanting to face it again. I empathized for the first time with my father. Slowly my body recovered from this nightmare. I lay there numbly in the dark anticipating the morning sunrise.

It was just three months ago that I withdrew a moderate sum of money and closed off my father's bank account. I recognized the bank manager from my high school. We chatted briefly and he offered his condolences. He was the stranger in my nightmare. But, why? I must have created this fear and paranoia that he was going to come after my money and kill my entire family. He knew I withdrew a substantial amount of money from his bank and knew my address.

In my nightmare, I was compelled to take action and kill my fears. Though these fears were never going to physically harm me, they created internal mental and emotional havoc. I felt helpless laying victim to these fears and so I killed them with a pen. The pen is symbolic of writing. Writing this book has proven to be very cathartic for me. It has heightened my awareness to my personal deep-seated fears that became fixed entities into my subconscious. These fears had molded my thoughts into unhealthy behaviors and have burdened my every way of life. Today I choose to free myself from all this emotional madness so that I can live happier and truly pursue a more peaceful existence.

Often I wonder if my Jewish community understands or acknowledges how they are personally afflicted by these fears and the harmful effects of harboring them as a collective group.

The squirrel learns to hoard its food to alleviate fear of the future, yet it also is one of the very few capable wild animals that can drop its defenses and fears and learn to trust people. Squirrels can be found eating from the hands of humans.

My father was never able to let down his defenses and his relationship to money mirrored the intensity of his fears. It was another evident reminder that he was imprisoned to his past his entire life.

Money was a tool to manipulate and control everyone around him and our family suffered immeasurably

My parents: Harriet and Arie Kaplan March 1954

FIVE

A Woman of Valor

A woman of valor, who can find? Her worth is far above jewels.
The heart of her husband trusts in her, and nothing shall he lack.
Book of Proverbs 31[1]

When my Orthodox friends in grammar school and high school invited me to their homes on Friday night, I would often listen to their dads read in Hebrew "The Woman of Valor" to their moms. I never heard my father recite this to my mother.

Under a tastefully designed, apricot-colored rose, floral chuppah (canopy), supported by four wooden poles with the sweet scented roses intertwined delicately around them, I stood dressed in a white, floor-length, ruffled, flared gown and an elbow-length, white-laced veil.

My straight, shoulder-length, dark-brown hair was styled into a soft and subtle eighties look. I have been told over the years by family

---

1 A Woman of Valor is a traditional poem which is usually recited by the husband to the wife before sitting down to the Friday night Shabbat meal with the family.

members that I was a glowing bride. Standing at five feet ten and slender, I was feeling beautiful and appropriately nervous. I stared forward at my rabbi for continued support and guidance during the ceremony.

Just one week prior to my wedding, I dreamt that I was standing under the chuppah, in my synagogue, waiting for my groom to stand by my side. While he was walking down the aisle toward me, I heard the beeping sound of his pager.

He stopped the ceremony, took out his pager from his tuxedo pants, and looked at the message. Then he looked straight at me and said, "Karen, I gotta go, my patient was just admitted into the hospital. Goodbye." In my dream he left me standing at the altar.

But on my wedding day, he was at my side wearing a black tail-coat tuxedo and looking slightly tense. I began fidgeting a bit because my lower back ached. It had started to hurt prior to the ceremony since I spent several hours standing and taking pictures with our wedding party while wearing this tightly fitted gown. Sitting was not an option, my gown would wrinkle. So I relieved my pain, temporarily, by leaning against walls until the ceremony began. At the altar I swayed from side to side.

Near the front of the synagogue sanctuary, off to the side of the aisle, were a flutist and violinist. I chose classic Hebrew love songs for the wedding party processional. As for me, I wanted to walk down the aisle to something different, bold and inspiring to mark this new period of my life. At twenty-three, I was anxious and ready to leave my home and marry. So as the doors opened to the sanctuary, I proudly made my entrance with one of my favorite melodies, the "Theme of Exodus". Yes, it seems a bit melodramatic, but it exudes a message of independence and triumph.

Under the chuppah, positioned at opposite sides were our parents, elegantly dressed and proudly standing close by, symbolically surrounding and supporting us as we embarked on our new journey in life. I glanced over at my beaming mother. She was filled with nachas, a sense of pride and joy, as she looked lovingly at me. My father had a even-keeled look; there was no smile and he seemed intently focused on every word emanating from the rabbi. The rabbi was nervous, yet immeasurably filled with honor and pride as he began to officiate at his baby sister's wedding.

Standing off to the sides of the chuppah were our seven bridesmaids, wearing cocktail dresses in the same shade of apricot as the flowers, plus seven tuxedoed groomsmen, who were our sisters, brothers, cousins, and dear friends. Though the synagogue sanctuary was filled to capacity with hundreds of guests whom I barely knew, it was an extraordinary sight. Even though my marriage ended seventeen years later in 2003, that moment in time was a cherished event for my entire family. As I reflected back on that day, I wondered what life was like for my mother when she married my father at age nineteen.

⸻

Thanksgiving 2010, was brutal, bone chilling and wet. It was the first time I left Chicago during the holiday season.

My ex-husband, Robert, and I alternate holidays with our children and this Thanksgiving was my turn to be with them. My friends call me the poster child of divorce because I ended it as civilly as possible. I tried to keep my children away from any fighting and kept the quarrels to a minimum. I filed for divorce citing "irreconcilable differences"; we lived like two ships in the ocean passing each other by and never communicating. Of course there were several rough patches during the divorce. I was forced to stand up for myself and demand an equitable settlement. I believe our children came out minimally scathed by the divorce. Robert and I to this day continue to maintain a convivial atmosphere for our children as we celebrate birthdays and graduations together at our homes with our extended families.

By this Thanksgiving, I was dating Bobby about a year and a half. My friends tease me for dating a man with the same name as my ex-husband, but my ex only cared to be called Rob or Robert and would correct anyone immediately for making that mistake.

At the last minute Bobby, about whom I will reveal more in a later chapter, invited my family to join him with his two children in Scottsdale, Arizona for the long weekend. Bobby likes to do things on the spur of the moment and my children and I gladly welcomed the escape to sunny warm Arizona. Coincidentally, for the past couple of months, I intended to contact Bella Kazen, my mother's third cousin to interview for this book. She happened to live in Scottsdale and finally after months of pro-crastinating, I called her the week before I left. Bella and I talked when my father died and soon after I decided to write a book. I wanted to inter-view her but time seemed to slip by as I was busy working, helping Noah prepare and pack for his freshman year at the University of Illinois and happily attending my daughter's varsity tennis matches after school and weekends. Max was studying at the University of Maryland finishing up his senior year and flew in to be with all of us in Arizona.

Cousin Bella lived minutes away from where we stayed in Scottsdale. She was my mom's lifelong confidant. I wanted to learn more about my parent's relationship early on in their marriage and I was certain she would disclose some vital information. Although I was very eager to gain more clarity, I was apprehensive since I was unsure what might unfold.

My Grandpa Max (my mother's father) was Bella's great-uncle. Back in the 1920s, Max sponsored her father so that he could immigrate to this country. Since then the two families remained very close growing up together on the west side of Chicago.

"I loved your mother," Bella said and smiled. "She was a wonderful woman with a big heart. Harriet and I were just two months apart and the best of friends. Every Sunday afternoon I looked forward to our families getting together. Your mom and I would play dolls and Monopoly when we were little and during those hot summer nights, our families would have overnighters in Douglas Park. We went to Marshall High School, married and had children at the same time. There was never a week that passed without talking or seeing one another."

Bella is a 76-year-old highly energetic, charismatic vivacious blonde with sparkling blue eyes. She is very personable, caring and candid. She holds nothing back and says exactly what is on her mind.

"Bella," I said, "I want you to divulge everything you can remember about my parents' marriage. Don't worry about hurting my feelings. I am fully aware of their secrets."

Bella sighed and said, "Fine, I will share everything that I know."

"Can you tell me how they met?" I asked.

"Your father and mother met at a B'nai B'rith dance on the west side of Chicago. At that time, your dad became very sick with a bleeding ulcer and your mother was at his bedside day and night in the hospital," she answered.

Bella said that my dad called Harriet a "good woman" for helping nurse him back to health and soon thereafter, my mother (just nineteen) married my father. My mother thought he was twenty-eight years old at the time, but later found out he was actually thirty-two.

Bella continued, "We tried to double date with your parents, but your father refused. He demanded that Harriet stay home to cook for him. You already know how your father hated to spend money in restaurants."

I nodded.

"Arie expected dinner and your mother had to prepare it on time for him every day," she bitterly explained. "He would be cursing her in Yiddish as he was coming up the stairs to their apartment demanding that the food be hot and ready."

(As Bella spoke, I recalled the repertoire of Yiddish curses my father used in our home. It was part of the daily conversations in our house. When he was in a humorous mood he would often say to my brothers "Gai kaken oifen yam" which literally means "go shit in the ocean" but he was just telling them to get lost. When my brothers asked him for money or a ride to a friend's house, he would tell them, "Ich vel dir geben kadoches" (I'll give you nothing) though the exact translation means "I'll give you malaria or a fever." To my mother he would say, "Geharget zolstu veren" (you should get killed) but it was just another phrase to say "drop dead." Sometimes he would shout, "Feif oif der," (I despise you). He had special curses for our neighbors such as "Gei in dr'erd mit kinder zizamen," (go to hell and take your children with you) or "afinster in yohr afdir" (you should have a black year). Once my mother received a call from the vice principal of Ida Crown Academy, our private Jewish high school; he said that Barry swore at one of his teachers in class. Barry said that the Rabbi was picking on him because he did not do his homework so he yelled back and said, "A geshvir dir in tuchas," (you should get an abscess up your rear end).)

One afternoon when Bella was in the apartment, she mindlessly touched the mail that was neatly arranged on the table. My mother immediately told her to leave it alone since he likes it placed a certain way. "He controlled her every move," Bella told me.

Soon, however, my mom was forbidden to take in the mail from the locked mail box. Bella said, "If your mom needed new shoes, he nixed it. He said the money was only for food. When she did not bring home enough groceries, he yelled at her, told to do better with the money next time."

To which I replied, "None of this is surprising."

(I knew how difficult my mother had it. When I was a child and went grocery shopping with my mom, she bought additional expensive food items and then returned them the next day to get some extra cash.)

Bella explained that one day my mom invited the entire family over and in front of everyone my father insulted my mother and said, "You are no good, rotten and stupid. You can't do anything right!"

"It was so painful to watch," Bella continued, "I wanted to tell him off but I was afraid of what he might to do your mom afterwards. So I hugged her and told her that I loved her and would always be there for her."

My heart felt heavy and I was mortified to realize that the entire family knew everything. My mother's life with my father was miserable. I suppressed my emotions; I was afraid that Bella would not be forthright if I appeared upset. Besides, I committed myself to this entire interview and wanted to hear as many details as possible.

"Early on in their marriage, your father had a small, part-time job working at a synagogue. Your mother wondered how he could 'daven' (pray) all day there. I knew he was an Orthodox man, so I asked him what he does all day long at the synagogue."

"Your father grinned and said that it was none of my business. If I knew, then the whole world would know."

"One time," Bella continued, "your mother called frantically worried about Arie since it was past 7:30 p.m. and he was not home yet. She thought something terrible may have happened to him. She was about to call the police when he walked into the apartment. So she asked him what happened. He yelled, 'don't worry about me', and then he went into his bedroom and slammed the door."

I remember my father mentioning an old man with whom he studied Torah sometimes in the evening. Bella looked at me with a knowing smile, "Keep listening, Karen. I'm trying to explain something here."

She continued on with another story, "Then there was another time when he didn't bother to come home at all. Your mother called the police and asked some relatives to help look for him."

"I vaguely remember," I said. "I must have been around eight or nine years old at that time."

"Well, at 7:00 a.m. the next morning, your cousin spotted him walking into the synagogue. He needed to be there for the morning 'minyan' (prayers). He was sleeping with another woman."

She stopped talking and looked at me briefly. She saw that I knew about his behavior. "I was so disgusted with your father's behavior and pleaded to your mother to leave him."

"What did she say?" I asked, seething inside. I realized then that my mother knew all about my father's affairs and I was devastated that everyone in my family knew, as well. I could barely contain the thought of my own mother facing him day after day knowing that he was sleeping around.

"Karen, I wanted your mother to divorce him. She felt that she had no where to go. She was too embarrassed to tell her own mother.

She wouldn't even show your Bubbie Rae the worn out shoes she wore and took them off before she stepped inside her apartment. There was no way she could say that he was a philanderer. Your mother could not raise three young children without any money; she thought her only choice was to stay with him. She said that at least Arie came home and provided for the family."

I could feel my heart racing now and I started to stir in my chair.

Then Bella added, "Karen, your mother hung on to that one little thread, she knew about his affairs but your father didn't care. He knew she would never leave him."

My chest and upper body cavity were tightening. Resentment and anger were building up inside of me and I tried to conceal it from her. "I advised Harriet to get a job so she could become more independent," said Bella, "She started working but your father demanded her to hand over her weekly paycheck. I told your mom to fight him and cash her own checks. But it was no use, he always won."

By now Bella was agitated. "I remember when Harriet was too sick to go to work and your father forced her out of bed and out the door. He did not want to lose a day's worth of pay," she nearly spat. My mother's day-to-day life was full of utter misery.

"I also encouraged her to get a driver's license and she did. But she was only allowed to use the car for grocery shopping. I thought I was helping her out by advising her to become more independent," Bella said.

"You were helping her," I said.

"He was obnoxious," she commented, "he believed he had all the answers and his viewpoints were golden and everyone else was stupid. He fought with his neighbors, who frequently called the police to resolve situation after situation at their apartments in East and West Rogers Park."

Then she said something that startled me. I gasped at her words.

"He was like a Hitler. He did everything in his power to control her. He never helped her carry the groceries up the stairs, never picked up a dish in the house and never bothered taking care of you and your brothers. She stood in the kitchen on her swollen feet all day cooking and cleaning, while raising three children on her own. He was never around to lift a finger," she sighed and in an anguished voice said, "and he did not love her."

For a Jew, a family member to compare my father, a Holocaust survivor, to Hitler was shocking, but she nailed who he had become, a despot. "Your mother was imprisoned by him," she added, "she was abused and battered."

Bella continued on with more stories but I couldn't listen anymore. I had enough. So I asked her, "Did my father have any redeeming qualities?"

"Yes," said Bella and her mood changed, "your father provided a strong Jewish education for all you children. He also encouraged all of you to become professionals and he paid for all your college tuition."

(Since elementary school, my brothers and I understood the importance of receiving a college education. Howard studied at the Skokie Yeshiva to become an Orthodox rabbi, received his degree in Accounting from the University of Illinois in Chicago (UIC) and his Master's degree in Finance from DePaul University. Barry studied architecture at UIC and received his Master's degree in Urban Planning from the University of Chicago. My bachelor's degree was from UIC in Nutrition.)

Toward the end of the interview, Bella's demeanor changed again. Her eyes became watery and she spoke somberly, "Her last years were very difficult. She began to feel weak and Arie was never around day or night. She knew he was having another affair."

(I could not fathom the extent of my mother's pain knowing that my father committed adultery during their entire marriage. While my dad was in the nursing home during the last eight months of his life, I would pick up Beba and drive her to visit him. One day while I was in the car returning from the nursing home with Beba, I asked her about her life in Russia and when she immigrated into the United States. She explained, "I arrived with my husband in 1993. In 1994 he passed away from prostate cancer."

"I'm sorry, that must have been difficult," I said. "So where and when did you meet my father?"

"I wanted to learn English so I took some classes at the Ark. That is where I met Arie in 1995. We ate there together at their weekly dinner for those who didn't have enough food." Her eyes twinkled and she reached over to pat my arm, remembering happier times. "He wanted to go out with me. He was very persistent," Beba said.

"Your father told me that he was all alone with his kids since his wife died and was interested in having a relationship. I finally gave in and went out with him. We have been together since," she said with a smile.

Then she asked me a question, which caught me off guard. "When did your mother die?"

I did not want to answer. There was no need to upset her. So I said, "Didn't my father tell you?"

She said, "No" and again she repeated the question waiting for a response. I had no choice but to tell her the truth. "My mother died August 7, 1997," I replied.

Her jaw dropped and a deafening silence filled the car. She turned away from me and stared out of her side window. We both remained quiet for the rest of the car ride home, me feeling bad for Beba, and Beba for the first time knowing that she'd been deceived.

Though it seems hard to believe Beba never knew that my mother was alive when they first met, my father had a knack for compartmentalizing his life.)

It was at the end of the interview and cousin Bella was choked up and her tears were visible. "I miss your mother terribly," she cried. "I loved her. She was a kind, smart and beautiful woman who raised three wonderful children despite your father. It is hard for me to talk about her without feeling upset. She never deserved to be treated this way. She suffered her whole life married to him."

I couldn't hold back my tears. They came trickling down my cheeks, too. Forty-three miserable years of her life were spent married to my father. She knew that she had to make the best of the situation since she felt she had no place to go. Shalva, the Jewish agency for abused women, did not exist back then so a person suffering from abuse had to go outside the community. My mother lived during a time where women were obligated to be dutiful and loyal to their husbands, even to their own detriment; divorce was generally frowned upon. My mother was a captive in her own home never letting on to the outside world how deeply despairing she lived her life.

In spite of everything, my mom remained a "good woman". Her spirit was not tarnished. She never succumbed to being vindictive, bitter or hateful. She chose to be kind instead of hurtful, loving instead of vengeful. My mother was a battered woman and unable to take the necessary steps to escape from my father's abuse, but she kept her dignity and proudly rose (to the best of her abilities) and unconditionally loved all three of her children. She tried to protect us from my father's abuse and took the brunt of his rage by shielding us and creating a tolerable environment. She taught me the past does not need to dictate the future. Until the day of her death, I felt her undying love.

My father's past led him to behave and treat everyone quite differently. He chose to harm instead of help, and hate instead of love. Revenge was his motivation. My father taught me how not to treat other people.

SIX

Remember

"I marvel at the resilience of the Jewish people. Their best characteristic is their desire to remember. No other people have such an obsession with memory."
-Elie Wiesel

The Hebrew calendar is marked throughout the year with many holidays that incorporate and reiterate the theme of our obligation to remember our anti-Semitic oppressors that brought suffering and persecution to the Jewish people.

Years ago in high school, I heard this Jewish joke, which summarizes this theme of our oppression.

1. Remember our enemies
2. With God's help we triumphed
3. Let's eat!

Passover

My mother would pour scalding hot water over the kitchen countertops to disinfect, clean and kill every microorganism and wash away microscopic remnants of chametz, (leavened food) before Passover. Chametz is forbidden for a Jew to own, consume or derive any benefit during the Passover holiday. Therefore, Jews will search, burn, nullify and sell their chametz. The kitchen cabinets and refrigerator were emptied, cleaned and lined with aluminum foil.

Then two completely different sets of dairy and meat pots, pans, flatware and plates were placed in separate kitchen cabinets for the eight days of Passover.

I meticulously searched for junk food and any minute crumbs that might have been left over in my room, closets, clothes pockets and purse and threw it all away. My mom came in my room as I was searching underneath my bed and said, "Karen, you have been cleaning your room for hours, it's time to help me cook in the kitchen."

My brothers shared a bedroom and Howard took it upon himself to clean up their room. He took Passover very seriously. Barry was not interested in following the rules and never bothered to help. Then the night preceding the holiday, my father led my brothers and me on a customary search throughout the house with a candle, feather and bag. Barry dispersed ten pieces of bread crumbs throughout the house and I carefully swept them into the bag using the feather. Howard then recited the blessings for this ritual. When Howard turned thirteen years old, my father gave him the responsibility of leading this ritual and he gladly took over.

Barry, as always, managed to stir up some trouble. One year he forgot to make a list of where he placed the crumbs and so we kept on finding them all over the house during the course of the holiday. Barry thought it was amusing while Howard and I were annoyed with him. My father scolded him and slapped him in the behind. The morning after the search was completed; Howard put all the chametz outside in our backyard into our large metal garbage can and set it all on fire. One time the fire went out of control and the fire trucks came with their sirens roaring and put out the fire. After that year, Howard burnt the chametz in our small Weber grill.

My job was to put all unopened cans of food, cereal boxes and other kitchen staples into a separate pantry and seal it off. Then I would fill out a form that I received from school listing the chametz in our sealed cabinet and hand it over to the rabbi at my school. The rabbi would act as our agent and sell our chametz to a non-Jew so that we would not be considered owners of any leavened food products in our home. Once Passover ended, the rabbi bought it all the back and we became rightful owners of our chametz.

My mother would spend hours shopping at the butcher, fish market and grocery store for Passover foods. Then she would work non-stop for several days before Passover from dawn until she was too tired to lift a spoon, cooking gefilte fish and brisket, preparing the chicken soup and matzah balls, stuffing the kishke and baking her famous sponge cakes and a mass array of other traditional holiday foods.

My father never helped around the house and when he was home, he spent most of his time in his bedroom with the door closed.

In school I learned that if I even ate the smallest piece of chametz on Passover, the punishment would be karet, an early death or being spiritually cut off from my people in the "World to Come". I really was not sure what the "World to Come" meant as a child, but I was fearful and knew that I had to strictly adhere to these Passover rules.

Then came the Seder, where my family would all sit around the kitchen table that I set for the holiday. I used our best white tablecloth and placed the candlesticks, wine glasses, a Seder plate which contains special foods, and matzah on the table. Every family member had a "Haggadah" (Passover booklet) and a pillow on their chair. I polished the silver, double-checked that there were no water spots on the glasses and tried to fold the cloth napkins in a unique design. My father would lead the service and along with a festive dinner we would recall the miraculous event of the liberation of the Jews from bondage in Egypt. I couldn't wait for my turn to read the passages in Hebrew and sing all the songs that I learned in school. At the table I kept on looking ahead in the Haggadah to see when it would be my turn to perform for everyone. Being the youngest, I couldn't wait to sing the famous four questions.

When it was Barry's turn to read, he always fumbled the words and added his own amusing rendition to the story like "God brought us forth from Egypt, with a strong hand and an outstretched arm and with one finger, two toes and a cane." My father thought Barry was lazy, foolish and especially irreverent when he changed the ancient words that were written by our rabbis centuries ago. My father raised his arm as if he was about to strike him, pointed his index finger right in his face and sternly said, "I'm going to get you...you better watch out!"

When Barry and I were young, many people mistakenly thought we were twins, even though he was four years older than I. We have the same complexion, hair color and eyes. But our personalities are completely different. In elementary school, I was studious, dedicated and followed the rules. His teachers branded him as stupid and lazy; at that time they did not understand dyslexia. Barry is actually quite bright and creative but mostly he was mischievous, immature and inappropriate. His behavior at the Seder table reflected his inability to read.

Eventually Howard took over the responsibility of leading our family Seder. My mother never participated. She could not read or speak Hebrew and by the time we all sat down to begin the Seder, she was thoroughly exhausted.

"B'chol dor vador, chayav adam lirot et atzmoh, ki elu who ya tza memitzraim."

This Hebrew quote read during the Seder means, "In every generation one must look upon himself as if he personally had gone out of Egypt."

Our rabbis commanded us to forge an emotional bond with our ancestors in Egypt so that we would remember their degradation and suffering. First my father told us to dip a piece of celery into a cup of salt water, recite the blessing and taste the tears of our ancestors. Then Howard told us to take a teaspoonful of bitter herbs or horseradish, which reminds us of the bitter times we endured as slaves, and eat it with "charoset" a mixture of chopped apples, walnuts and cinnamon. This mixture looks like mortar, so that we are reminded of the inhumane and torturous practices we were subjected to our Egyptian taskmasters while building the grand cities of the Egyptian empire. Howard made sure we ate an adequate amount of horseradish to remind us of the bitter taste of slavery, but I couldn't eat it; it tasted nasty. Matzah is poor man's bread, the bread of affliction that was eaten as the Hebrews hurriedly departed from Egypt. I loved eating the matzah, at least for the first few days of the holiday until it literally made me sick to my stomach.

As this monumental story comes to a close when God helped lead Moses, our prophet, to guide our newborn nation to freedom, we eagerly waited for our mother to bring the bountiful feast of food to the table. My father was always served first and expected his food, especially the chicken soup, to be piping hot. He sat at the head of the table watching my mother work like a slave and commanded her to bring him the salt or pepper at a moment's notice. He was very impatient and when he did not get what he wanted immediately, he bashed his fists on the table. Tension would begin to mount if the temperature of the food was not hot enough for him. My father seemed to enjoy my mother's cooking; we all did. Sometimes I would hear him say to himself under his breath that the food was very tasty, but I never heard him say thank you to my mother.

Sitting at the Seder table, I was always on edge wondering when a fight would erupt. My father randomly picked on one of my brothers and the Seder would end with my parents and brothers all screaming at each other. Then my mother would break down and cry. I would sit there watching the chaos and wishing it would all go away. It never did, so I left the table and went into my room leaving it all behind. All I wanted was to complete the Seder peacefully and sing the songs I learned from school. Rarely did that happen.

What I learned in school was the emotional bond created in the Seder is an attempt to help us connect to our ancestors who were victimized by Pharaoh, king of Egypt, who was considered our first anti-Semite at the birth of our nation. United by our past suffrage and victimization, we continue to expose these thought patterns and feelings onto our future generations, just as we have done habitually for over the past thousands of years.

As an adult, I insured that my home was strictly kosher for Passover and I was bogged down weeks before the holiday cleaning, shopping and cooking, just like my mother. During our Seder, I incorporated readings about the Holocaust and current world-wide anti-Semitism into the narrative. Gradually over the years, I began questioning all these observances. I felt disillusioned, confused and overwhelmed by all the work and not anticipating the holiday. Eventually, I realized that I can fully appreciate the story of the Exodus of our past without indulging in all this negativity. For me it is a reminder to fully embrace the blessings of our abundance, prosperity and freedom in the United States. We remember what is was like to be a stranger in a strange land and feel fully privileged to live in this land of freedom, free of physical and religious constraints.

I also realized that there is another part of this redemption process that is imperative to understand and fully integrate into our lives: that is, from the depths of slavery, the Hebrews became a free people. And while the physical chains of slavery were broken, the Hebrews were still enslaved psychologically and emotionally to Egypt. Born into a world of slavery, under the whips and chains of their taskmasters, slavery was the only life they recognized and their fear of change and of the unknown was debilitating and stifled them from fully embracing their new-found freedom. Leaving Egypt, wandering into the desert, an unfamiliar and frightful terrain must have seemed like an overwhelmingly physical and mental feat to pursue.

There was an unsettling comfort when they dwelled in Egypt, under the domination of Pharaoh. In Egypt they had a home and understood the expectations of their taskmasters. They left Egypt unable to fully shed their slave mentality, thus bringing all their fears and doubts along with them. They expressed their fears several times to Moses, wondered why God delivered them from bondage to die in the desert. Even after witnessing all of God's glorious miracles of redemption, they committed the sin of creating the golden calf to worship, instead of the praising the God that delivered them from slavery. The Hebrews understandably appeared spiritually handicapped and unable to connect with their God and enjoy their new found freedom.

I think that there are others who unconsciously indulge in their emotional pain of depression, guilt, anger or resentment, and suffer throughout their entire lives.

I made the connection that, like the Hebrews, my father was enslaved to his Holocaust experience, and never overcame those frightful years. Bound to the memories of his horrific experiences, he was incapable of enjoying his newfound freedom of life in the United States. He, too, was spiritually and emotionally handicapped.

My mother was enslaved to my father, who controlled and manipulated her throughout their marriage. She found solace in eating and so food became her friend and eventually her enemy. Her addiction to food satiated her temporarily and repressed her anger, discontent and confused feelings. A vicious cycle of emotional eating ensued and over the years she became morbidly obese.

She wasn't the only one to find relief in unhealthy behaviors and cover up her feelings. I've known relatives and friends who rely on alcohol, sex, shopping, prescription and nonprescription drugs, money, power, work and image to cover up their feelings.

I, too, was bound to my past. I alienated myself from my father and all of his meshugaas (craziness) as a child. He always seemed busy and inattentive so I never initiated any conversations with him. I avoided him during breakfast while he watched the news and purposely always sat in the back seat of the car busying myself with homework as he drove me to school. If he happened to walk into a room where I was sitting, I left. Never knowing when he would start yelling, I protected myself by keeping my distance from him. This was my coping mechanism and it worked. I could write an entire chapter about my father ignoring and emotionally abandoning me, but suffice to say he was emotional unavailable and I kept it that way with our distancing.

However, I unconsciously carried this behavior into my adult life and became emotionally distant from my husband. It was rather easy, since I married someone that mirrored me. He, too, was emotionally handicapped. To my friends and relatives, we may have seemed comfortable living in a lifeless and loveless relationship until I realized that I was miserable, depressed and lonely. So I worked with a therapist and read tons of self-help books. I encouraged him to try therapy, but he said that he was afraid of what he may find and he was satisfied with our relationship. I wanted change and thought that my only option was divorce.

My brother Barry to this day carries his anger within him and is unable to let go of the pain he endured as a child. I know this because he replays his memories in his mind over and over like a recorded video and tells me his anguished experiences of our childhood. He speaks as if our father had abused him last week though he has been dead for years. He, too, suffers and, unknowingly, is bound to his past.

If we as a collective group of people are asked generation upon generation to conjure up all these crippling feelings of our past and live our lives as if we have just survived the Exodus, we as people cannot be spiritually free. We have enslaved ourselves to our negative emotions of our past and have buried them alive within us. We truly have not mastered the real meaning of freedom. How can we honor our past and let go of our pain? How can I make sense of my disconsolate relationship with my father and move beyond the pain? How can I begin to heal? Delving into these very questions was the start of a journey to a better way of life.

Counting the Omer

Every day at school during morning prayers, my classmates and I would count the forty nine days between the second night of Passover and the next holiday called Shavuot, when God gave the Children of Israel the Torah. Historically, during the days of the Holy Temple, Jews offered a sacrifice of an omer, a measure of barley, for each of the forty-nine days representing the harvest season. The link between these two particular holidays is a reminder that the redemption from slavery was not complete until the Hebrews received God's law.

I never really enjoyed this interval because the rabbis transformed it into a period of mourning to commemorate the deaths of twenty four thousand students of Rabbi Akiva. Rabbi Akivah was one of the greatest spiritual leaders of the Jewish people. In 132 A.D., 24,000 of his students died from a plague, and Bar Kochba, the military leader at that time, failed to overrun the Romans. Rabbi Akivah was eventually captured, tortured and died as a martyr at the hands of the Romans. He said, "All my life I've been waiting to fulfill the concept 'You shall love God, with all your heart, with all your soul and with all your might' (Deuteronomy 6:5) and now I finally have the chance."

My friends and I couldn't listen to music nor have parties during these seven weeks. No one in our family would get haircuts and my father grew a beard since shaving was prohibited. Yet, the rabbis declared that there are occasional intermittent days when all the prohibitions are rescinded. May 4, 1986, was my wedding day and one of the few times during this spring interval in which all the rules of mourning are lifted and Howard permitted us to marry. To this day, many Jews in my community observe these strict rules to commemorate this tragic period of Jewish history.

Shiv'ah Asar B'Tammuz - **The 17th day of the month Tammuz**

Every summer, my Jewish community would commemorate the breaching of the walls of the Holy Temple of Jerusalem marking this day, the 17th of Tammuz, as the beginning of a three-week mourning period. The Holy Temple was first built on Mount Moriah, in the Old City of Jerusalem by King Solomon in 957 B.C. After its destruction in 586 B.C. by the Babylonians, it was rebuilt in 515 B.C. only to be destroyed in 70 A.D. by the Romans. It was the central place of ancient Jewish worship where daily animal sacrifices and prayer services were held. This day is a minor fast day, so eating and drinking are not allowed from sunrise to sunset.

When I was too young to fast, my teachers in grade school suggested that I avoid snacks and desserts on all the fast days as a way to commemorate the days. As a child, I remember when the Good Humor truck would come barreling down our block. From inside my house I could hear the "Ice Cream Man" jingling the bells and like a bolt of lightning all the neighborhood kids would run after him and surround the truck. On this fast day, I stood at my front door and watched the kids waiting in line for ice cream. I felt mighty and proud, knowing that I was doing the right thing and God would find favor in me for not snacking on ice cream.

This is also the day when Moses descended from Mt. Sinai carrying the first set of the Ten Commandments, witnessed the golden calf and smashed the tablets to the ground.

This three-week interval is considered a time of danger and misfortune. Major surgeries are postponed, traveling is prohibited and certainly no weddings or parties are planned. When I was young, I would not eat red meat or chicken and drinking wine was prohibited.

In August of 1991 during these three weeks, my mother and I were invited to a cousin's wedding shower and Howard didn't want us to go. My mother and I decided to go anyway and just a few weeks later Howard died. My mother said to me, "God cursed me for going to the party during the forbidden period."

Once again, the calendar marked another time period where we lived in the despair of our history.

Tisha B'Av - **9th day of Av**

"The city that was full of people is lonely now.
The city is like the wife of a dead husband.
Once she was great.
She was like a queen among the other places in the country.
Now she is a slave.
She weeps in the night and there are tears on her face.
Not one of her lovers will help her to feel better.
All her friends have left her.
They have gone against her and they are now her enemies.
The people's enemies rule them now.
Those who hate them have plenty.
The Lord has caused trouble for the people because they did so many wrong
things the enemies took the children away to work as slaves."

-Lamentations

Every year on the ninth of Av, I would meet my school friends at their synagogue. Our family never belonged to a synagogue since my father always worked at various synagogues in the community. My friends and I would sit on a low stool or on the floor reciting the psalms from "Eicha" the Book of Lamentations. This is the saddest day of the Jewish calendar. It is the day when the Babylonians destroyed the first Holy Temple of Jerusalem and the Romans destroyed the second Holy Temple. The expulsion of the Jews from Spain and other Jewish catastrophes occurred on this tragic day.

This holiday falls in the middle of summer when the days are long and the heat can be intense. Nothing would deter me from fasting twenty-five hours without food or liquids on this day. When I turned twelve, I couldn't wait to prove myself as an adult member in my community and fast. This was my rite of passage. Before sunset, my brothers and I would eat a huge meal and then meet our friends at synagogue. Barry usually snuck away from services and ended up at a neighbor's house. He never cared to fast. My Jewish community gathered, prayed and mourned over the destruction of Jerusalem and our Holy Temple. By the end of the fast, my mouth was dry, my lips were parched, and my head was throbbing.

When I was at summer overnight camp, I remember sitting at the shores of the lake with all my camp friends on the eve of the 9th of Av. It was pitch dark outside and in the middle of the lake we witnessed a small wood hut standing on a barge going up in flames. As we watched the reenactment of the burning of the Temple, the entire camp sang this melancholy song in Hebrew and English,

"Down by the waters of Babylon,
We lay down and cried for thee Zion.
We remember, thee remember, we remember thee Zion."

As soon as the fire died, another barge with four Hebrew letters spelling the Hebrew word "zachor", meaning "to remember" went up in flames.

I mourned on Tisha B'Av as if I was grieving the death of a loved one.

At the end of my wedding ceremony, Howard held up a glass wrapped up in a white cloth and said, "The shattering of this glass serves as a memorable expression of the destruction of both of the Holy Temples of Jerusalem."

This is a cherished custom usually marking the end of the marriage ceremony. Howard then shared something that I have never heard at a wedding before. "It is also incumbent upon us, the children of Holocaust survivors, to remember the Holocaust. We cannot forget what has happened to our father's family and to this past generation of Jews. We have a responsibility to repopulate the lost six million Jewish victims."

He placed the cloth on the floor near my husband, who then stomped on it and broke the glass.

During my childhood, there were always cutting reminders of the destruction of the Holy Temple in my home. My mother tried saving some money to buy a new kitchen table and chairs and settled for a damaged glass table that was partially chipped at the corner. When we sat around the table for dinner, Barry sarcastically remarked, "This defective table with cracked glass serves as a symbol for our family to remember the destruction of the Holy Temple."

Our bitter Jewish history always managed to penetrate throughout the mundane and cherished moments of my childhood and into my adult life. I loyally continued to conjure up the painful past of my Jewish ancestry.

Tzom Gedalia - **Fast of Gedaliah**

By the time I was an upper classman in high school, the thrill of fasting had worn off but I continued to dutifully observe our sorrowful past. In early autumn, school was in session and another fast day was implemented by the rabbis to lament the assassination of Gedaliah, the Jewish governor, who was appointed by the Babylonian king after 586 B.C. Yishmael Ben Netaniah, a Jewish royal descendant murdered him and the Jews that remained under King Nebuchadnezzar's rule were fearful of his retaliation and swiftly fled the country.

In high school, most of the teachers and students fasted on this day. Everyone seemed to lack luster by the afternoon. Gym and music classes were canceled and by 5:30 p.m., which is when the school day ended, I was anxious to go home and break the fast at sunset.

Mar Cheshvan

In late autumn, the Hebrew month of Cheshvan arrives without a single holiday or fast day to observe. I learned in school that the rabbis coined this month as "mar" Cheshvan, meaning a "bitter" month. I was always puzzled why they thought this month was bitter because my mother finally had a break from preparing for holidays and I was relieved there were no fast days.

You may start to wonder, 'what is the point of enumerating all these mournful periods and fast days?' As I looked back at the Jewish calendar, I discovered that my childhood life was preoccupied by my dismal history; eventually, it dampened my spirit.

Hanukah

The smell of fried "latkes" (potato pancakes) filled the air in our home during these eight nights of Hanukah. My mother would stand and grate potatoes and onions and make the most delicious latkes. That was a miracle for me because in addition to working all day on her feet, she would day after day prepare dinner and during Hanukah she even surpassed herself. We topped the latkes with apple sauce and sour cream and devoured them as quickly as she put them on the serving plate. As a child, I learned to play the traditional game of dreidel, a spinning top with four sides. My brothers and I lit the Hanukah menorah each of the eight nights at home.

When I was eleven years old, my mother saved up some money and bought me an old, used piano. I loved playing the piano. First I would practice my classical music and then I would spend hours teaching myself to play Hebrew folk songs and prayers. My mother was my sole audience and as much as I loved playing and singing for her, she enjoyed listening to me. When I was older, I continued to play and added music from other genres of folk, rock and contemporary music. I especially loved Simon and Garfunkel, Barry Manilow and Barbra Streisand.

During Hanukah, I played and sang the songs each night after lighting the menorah. My brothers always joined me in singing and we began with the traditional song called "Maot Tzur," (Rock of Ages). This song describes the innate theme of the triumph over the four ancient enemies of Israel with the aid of God.

After dinner when my father went into his bedroom, my mother secretly handed my brothers and me a small gift and some chocolate "gelt" or coins. We all knew to hide our gifts and avoid any unnecessary conflict with our father since he considered gift giving to be frivolous.

In grade school I learned the standard but not completely accurate version of the Hanukah story which commemorates the Jewish victory over the Seleucid Empire in 165 B.C. and the rededication of the Holy Temple of Jerusalem. In this version, another evil tyrant, King Antiochus, desecrated the Holy Temple, Hellenized the Jewish people and attempted to destroy the culture. But the mighty Maccabees revolted and reduced the influence of Hellenism. I learned that the victory over the Seleucid Empire came through God's intervention and truly believed the legend regarding the miracle of the temple oil which should have burned one night but lasted eight nights.

Several years ago, I learned the full truth about what transpired during this vulnerable period of Jewish history. The fact is that there was civil unrest between the traditional Jews, who were fiercely determined to keep the the laws of the Torah, and the Hellenized Jews, who wanted to assimilate into the Greek culture.

Matthias, a rural priest, and the armed Maccabees of Modi'in were fearful of the extermination of Judaism. They turned against the

Hellenized Jews by terrorizing and murdering them. Our fears led us to a bloody, civil war pinning Jew against Jew. The Hellenized Jews sought protection from Antiochus and the battle between the Maccabees and the Seleucid armies ensued.

Today, much like two thousand years ago, especially noticeable in Israel, there is a polarization of the Jewish people. The Haredi or Ultra Orthodox Jews and the secular Jews continue to clash with each other and history seems to be repeating itself.

Tenth of Tevet

Hanukah is barely over and another minor fast day appears on the Jewish calendar. The tenth of Tevet commemorates the siege of Jerusalem by the Babylonian king. My brother Howard, the budding Rabbi, was always a serious and committed Jew. He would wake up early before the sunrise and eat and then fast until sunset. As a young child, I admired my big brother and tried to be as committed as he was, but I was never as good at it. After I graduated high school from Ida Crown Jewish Academy, these minor fasts went first and I slowly stopped fasting while everyone in my community faithfully remembered this tragic day.

Not even the Chief Rabbi of Israel choosing this day to be a "general Kaddish day" or a day of mourning for the unknown murdered victims of the Holocaust was enough to inspire devotion from me once I lost my original fervor.

Purim

I hardly remember celebrating Purim. Other children went to Purim carnivals and dressed up in costume for the reading of the Scroll of Esther, but my father was always busy working in the synagogue and my mother was never comfortable going to services where she did not have a membership. The Scroll of Esther is a Hebrew text chanted on the eve of Purim and the following morning and I learned that I must hear every single word. During this holiday, I do remember helping my mother bake hamantaschen, (triangle shaped pastries) with "mohn" or poppy seed filling which my father loved best.

When I had children, I made sure we celebrated the holiday so that they would enjoy the synagogue carnivals. My sons would dress up as Power Rangers, Teenage Mutant Ninja Turtles, super heroes, the king of Persia and even Haman, the evil character of Purim. My daughter masqueraded as queens of Egypt and Persia. One year I dressed her as an M&M hamantaschen.

At the latter end of winter, Jews celebrate this holiday by listening to the story in the Scroll of Esther, sending gifts to friends, giving charity and, of course, eating a festive meal. Our attention is geared toward Haman, the notorious anti-Semite whose lineage stems from the evil nation called the Amalekites of the biblical period.

As a child I assumed this story was true. The setting occurs in Persia where Haman, the king's prime minister, plotted to exterminate the Jews and influenced King Achashverosh to issue edicts all over the kingdom to eradicate them. At the end of the Scroll miraculously the Jewish people are saved through the invisible power of God with the aid of the pious Jew, Mordecai, and his niece, the beautiful and ravishing Queen Esther.

As the Scroll of Esther was recited in the congregation, my children would masquerade in costumes and use "greggers" (noisemakers) to blot out the name of this evil man, Haman, as he is mentioned. We are also encouraged to drink to delirium until we cannot distinguish between the wicked Haman and the benevolent Mordecai.

"Zachor," to remember, is a commandment found in the Torah for every generation of Jews to remember the cowardly attacks of the barbaric nation of Amalekites. In school I learned that when the tired and weakened Israelites departed Egypt and crossed the Red Sea, they inadvertently encroached on the territory of the Amalekites. The Amalekites attempted to massacre the Israelites by approaching from behind and killing the woman and children first.

My teachers explained that Haman is a direct descendant from Amalek and we must erase his name from history. To properly fulfill this commandment, we must hear the public reading of the Chapter Zachor from the Torah every year on the Sabbath which precedes Purim. We are obligated to remember our enemies.

Later on in my adulthood, I learned the truth from my Rabbis that this riveting and suspenseful story of Purim was fictitious. It was instituted as a fixed holiday into the Jewish calendar during the Maccabean period; hundreds of years after the Jews lived in Persia. Haman the anti-Semite never existed, nor did Mordecai or Esther. There is no historical evidence documenting that a Persian king by the name of Achashverosh married outside the royal dynasty to a commoner, a Jewish woman named Esther. We assumed this story to be genuinely true, since it fervently validates the ongoing theme of anti-Semitism and oppression of the Jewish people.

The Jewish people were exiled to Babylon from Judea by King Nebuchadnezzar, in the sixth century BC. The Jews were desolate, yet desperately hopeful that one day they would return to their homeland and rebuild the Temple in Jerusalem. Soon thereafter, Persia conquered Babylon, and life improved remarkably for the Jews. The Persian King treated the Jews well, giving them full and welcomed autonomy to remain in Persia or return to their homeland to rebuild their Temple.

This fun-filled creative narrative was especially critical to the psyche of the Jews during the Maccabean revolt. It mentally uplifted their spirits and strengthened their hopes of salvation at a morose period in history.

The Jews celebrated the deaths of the evil tyrant, Haman, his entire family, and 75,000 Persian enemies who attempted to annihilate them. Just as people from all over the world masquerade and celebrate Carnival, Mardi Gras and Halloween, Jews disguise themselves, drink to confusion and put on Purim Shpiels (slapstick plays) to engage in merry-making. It is thought that Jews began masquerading in the late 1400s when the Italian Jews were influenced by the Roman Carnival.

Purim reminds me of the movie *Inglorious Bastards* which seemed to me like a fantasy film for Holocaust survivors and their descendants. The successful plot killing Hitler and the Nazis was a thrilling and indulging fantasy for Jews to watch on the big screen.

In the scroll of Esther, the royal marriage of Esther to Achashverosh was never discussed in all my years of Hebrew day school education.

Esther's intermarriage with the King was an integral and key part of the Jewish survival in this story of Purim. Esther influenced him to help save her and her people from mass destruction. But when I was taught to believe that this story is non-fiction, the fear of assimilation lingered and there would be no discussion of the value of this royal marriage.

Yom Hashoah - **Holocaust Day**

"I believe with complete faith in the coming of the Messiah, and, though he may tarry, I wait daily for his coming."

Every year on Holocaust Day, I sang these words in Hebrew to a melancholy melody during school assemblies, synagogue services and at home as I played the piano. The song was sung by Jewish concentration camp prisoners as they were herded into the gas chambers, as related by Jews assigned to work the ovens.

Holocaust Day, which occurs in the springtime, is the day we commemorate the victims of the Holocaust. Those who were willing to speak about their past would share their tales of survival. We would recite special readings and prayers in the synagogue and light six candles to remember the six million.

Growing up in my household, it was implicitly understood that the world was, is and will always be anti-Semitic. Anytime my father would speak about Hitler and the Holocaust it was predicated with hatred and disgust for the people of Europe. They were all "no good", he would say as he lectured me to take every precaution when dealing with the outside world. I was to trust no one, because he considered every European as a potential Nazi.

My entire community, not just my father, considered anyone who spoke against Jews or Israel to be anti-Semitic. God forbid, if a Jew ever spoke out against a "landsman", he was labeled a self-hating Jew.

Even our voting patterns were a reflection of the past. My father and my community taught me to always vote for a Jew running for office and vote only for the non-Jew who has shown commitment to being a friend of Israel.

My Jewish community in the 1960s and 70s was relentless about exposing the evils of the Holocaust to the next generation of Jews. In school when I was young, I began reading children's books on the Holocaust. The weekly Jewish magazine *The Sentinel* was one of the many publications appearing on our kitchen table filled with articles covering every imaginable angle of the war and anti-Semitism. At high school assemblies and community events, I listened to countless speeches from

Jewish historians and scholars, noted Nazi hunters and authors detailing the coverage of World War II and the current waves of anti-Semitism in our community and worldwide.

Organizations and memorials specifically focusing on anti-Semitism and the Holocaust were cropping up all over the world so that Jews would never forget the genocide of our people. My father spearheaded an organization called "FOR THE SIX MILLION MARTYRS - NATIONAL CULTURAL MEMORIAL ASSOCIATION" which attempted to build a monument in Chicago in memory of the six million deaths. I remember the picture of him at City Hall in 1967 from *The Sentinel*. He was standing next to the old Mayor Daley of Chicago and several Chicago Aldermen who shared his ambitious dream of creating a Chicago memorial. Of course the attempt collapsed when my father alienated the entire committee. As he tried to control everyone and every decision made at the meetings, the committee members left. The organization dwindled and eventually he used the money for his personal needs. No one ever knew he was stealing the money since he had control of the financial records and the bank accounts. I remember him handing me checks from this organization to pay for my school supplies. At the time, I never understood what he was actually doing.

In my private Jewish high school, part of the curriculum was a mandatory class on Jewish history spanning the last 2,500 years of our ancestry. Many of my teachers were Holocaust survivors and they heavily influenced my perspective of the world. At school, I also took part in an extracurricular program for students who were children of Holocaust survivors. In this program all we did was read about and discuss the Holocaust. The appendix indicates just a few of the programs for Holocaust education in my community and worldwide.

My father immersed himself in reading books about the Holocaust until he reached the middle of his eighties and his perceptions were so distorted from dementia that reading was impossible. Barry didn't read much except for comic books, but Howard was an avid reader of Jewish history. He could answer any question in detail about any time period and was especially preoccupied with World War II. My mother was quite content reading romance fiction on Saturday mornings while we were all at services.

I believe our world still needs to learn and explore the grim details of the Holocaust and other genocides that have occurred since then. But the inundation of Holocaust education has weighed me down burdening my life with hatred and fear.

Several years ago I asked my father if he would like to submit his testimony with Steven Spielberg. He said' "don't bother me with nareshkeit (foolishness). There is nothing for me to gain by doing that." He then walked away and muttered under his breath some curse in Yiddish. A few years later when my synagogue was videotaping survivors I thought he might have changed his mind as he aged. He wasn't interested.

For over two decades, I just avoided movies, books and news articles. I skipped it all. No matter how popular the movie, I didn't want to see it. I was busy raising my three young children and used this job as a reason to avoid contact.

To this very day, my Jewish community continues to immerse itself in the barbaric events of the Holocaust, steadfast and determined to understand and preserve every aspect of the Holocaust.

We tenaciously remember prewar Nazi Germany, the Nuremberg laws, and Kristallnacht. We remember Nazi occupation of Europe, the pogroms, the ghettos, the hidden children and converted children. We remember Nazi extermination camps, the human experiments and Dr. Mengele's Jewish twin experiments. We remember the gas chambers and the death squads. We remember Jewish resistance and the partisans. We attempt to remember every victim's and every survivor's story.

We want our bar mitzvah age children, college youth, and adults to absorb the gruesome stories of our past and remember the pain of our ancestors. We must remember! We intentionally carry these abominable details, feel them and forever implant them into our psyche and continue to teach them diligently to the next generation.

Zachor!

"In Jewish history there are no coincidences," quoted Elie Wiesel, author, peace activist, Nobel Prize Laureate and Holocaust survivor. Although I now understand that there are no coincidences in the world, as a child I was too overburdened by the continuous flow of painful suffering to do anything but internalize it. Instead of enjoying the innocent view of the world as kind, I already incorporated a bitter consciousness of hatred, bigotry and darkness. Even if I wanted to escape from the continuous down pouring of Holocaust imagery, I was tormented by the possibility of being disloyal. I carried a burden of stress and paranoia on my little shoulders along with constant fear.

I think my personal experience coincides with that of the greater Jewish community. There are of course exceptions and those who managed to separate themselves, but Judaism in general carries a blueprint of "scapegoatism" that continues to affect both its followers and those who pull apart.

I can't help but wonder if we have learned the deeper lessons behind what history has presented to us. Or if we have generation upon generation continuing to unconsciously follow the same thought patterns of our ancestors by diligently remembering our oppressive past and allowing that past to stagnate our behaviors.

Israel Independence Day

Israel has created a new image of the Jew in the world - the image of a working and an intellectual people, of a people that can fight with heroism.
    - David Ben-Gurion, (first Prime Minister of Israel)

After centuries of persecutions, expulsions and virulent anti-Semitic attacks, the Jews finally returned to their ancestral homeland of Israel. When World War II ended, the newly formed United Nations voted to divide the British Mandate of Palestine into two states, one for the Jews and one for the Arabs.

The Jews accepted the U.N. plan and the State of Israel was born on May 15, 1948, when the mandate ceased. The Arab world rejected the plan and attacked the Jews the very next day by all the surrounding neighbors: Egypt, Jordan, Saudi Arabia, Iraq, Syria and Lebanon.

Years before Israel became a state, my Aunt Tova was preparing to leave Poland and settle in Palestine. In 1939 she attained her legal papers and traveled throughout Istanbul and Beirut, finally reaching Palestine within the year. She married Chaim Tzur in 1940 and they both volunteered in the Jewish Brigade of the British Army fighting against the Nazis in 1942. Tova was a nurse while Chaim was a soldier and both served in Egypt, Malta and Italy.

They also helped smuggle the Jewish refugees from Eastern Europe into Palestine since immigration was blocked by the British. Chaim continued on to fight in Austria and France. After the World War II ended in 1945, they both returned to Palestine and settled in a small town called Rishon L'Tzion and had two sons, Tali and Avi.

In the early 1950s on "Kol Yisrael" (Israeli radio), names of Holocaust survivors were announced each day at 1:00 p.m. sharp for ten minutes. Survivors all across the world were searching for living relatives in Israel. My Aunt Tova was home ironing one day when she heard my father's name announced on the radio and fainted. She sent a telegram to my father in the United States and discovered that he was the only survivor of their family. Tova suggested that he remain in the United States; life was difficult in Israel and they both believed that America would create more opportunities and a better way of life for him.

Something changed in the psyche of the Jews living in Israel after the Holocaust. As the 1948 War of Independence ensued they defended their piece of land as the survival of their nation again was tested. They understood that a victim-like mentality would not enable them to exist. So they shed the submissive, meek and fearful patterns of the Eastern European Jews and unwavering thoughts of pride, hope, strength and indestructibility emerged. The new image of the fearless, Israeli Jew was created. Tova's younger son Avi, about whom I will have more to say in a later chapter, said, "Our education was based on slogans like "Masada shall never fall again" and "we will never again be sacrificed like sheep or cattle."

Avi was referring to when the Roman troops in 72 A.D. sieged Masada, an isolated plateau overlooking the Dead Sea in the Judaean Desert, which led to the mass suicide of 960 Jews. The "never again" comment is a motto surfaced by the modern-day Jew. The Jews during the Holocaust had no army, navy or air force to protect them from the Nazis and vowed that they will never again be killed without a fight.

I was always interested in the Exodus story and tried to understand why it took forty years of preparation for the Hebrews to occupy Canaan, the promised land of their forefathers. My interpretation is that when the Hebrews left Egypt, they were not mentally capable of conquering the land of Canaan and so they wandered in the desert forty additional years, birthing a new generation of warriors.

God spoke to Moses in the plains of Moab by Jordan at Jericho, saying, "Speak unto the children of Israel and say unto them: When you pass over the Jordan into the land of Canaan, you shall drive out all the inhabitants of the land before you and destroy all their figured stones and their molten images and demolish their high places. You shall drive out the inhabitants of the land and dwell there, for unto you I have given this land to possess." Numbers 33:50-53

These young Israelite warriors came together during the forty years in the desert as a powerful and fearless army of the region. We know this because of Joshua's description of the conquest of Canaan as he defeated the kings and captured the cities. Joshua 11:16-12:24

The modern-day Israelites masterfully learned to defend themselves against the much larger Arab population. When the collective consciousness of the Jewish people changed and they no longer were enslaved to their victim mentality, they proved that they could overcome immense obstacles. They survived The War of Independence in 1948, the Sinai War of 1956, the Six day War of 1967, the Yom Kippur War of 1973, the Lebanon War in 1982, and two intifadas-and they continue to survive suicide bombings and daily rocket attacks from Gaza.

To show my solidarity with the State of Israel, as a child on Israel Independence Day, I would raise money and participate in the city-wide "Walk for Israel". My friends and I along with thousands of Jews walked miles through the Chicago neighborhoods proudly waving the Israeli flag and singing songs feeling like we were doing something important.

In school, all the teachers and students wore white tops and blue skirts or pants. We began our assemblies with Hatikvah, the Israeli national anthem and marked this day with special ceremonies and eating falafel, hummus and pita sandwiches for lunch.

America, the "melting pot" of immigrants from different countries, races and religions, is my home. I feel privileged and blessed that my father and mother's family were permitted to enter, work and live freely among its citizens. Yet, resonating within me since childhood was a deep-seated fear that one day America will turn its back on Jewish citizens and our ugly, oppressive history will repeat itself once again.

Because of this ingrained fear, the country of refuge, my home away from home, has always been the State of Israel. Many American Jews feel this way.

All the anti-Semitic atrocities my father experienced during the Holocaust were his identity throughout his life. He could not and would not break away from the horrors of his past and remained a victim to it. My father could not even escape his trauma while asleep; he had night terrors until he died. He was never at peace.

From a very young age, my family and religious life were centered on the suffering and annihilation of my relatives, ancestors and people. My identity as a Jew was defined by fearing and confronting the anti-Semitism coursing through generations of my people shaping my relationship with my religion and God.

The quote from the Passover Seder "In every generation one must look upon himself as if he personally had gone out of the Egypt" could have easily substituted the word Holocaust for Egypt.

"In every generation one must look upon himself as if he personally had gone out of the Holocaust."

Our family did not need to taste the bitter herbs, salt water or charoset as a reminder of the suffering of our ancestors. We sensed, smelled, tasted and breathed the bitterness and pain of our people each and every day. As a result, my father's Holocaust became our family's Holocaust. As I worked with therapists and spiritual counselors over the years, I discovered how deeply affected I was by my father's trauma.

I, too, vowed to never forget and I, too, hated Germans and Poles. I, too, directed my life toward the security and safety of the Jewish people. I considered myself a Child of a Holocaust Survivor and another victim. That was my identity in life.

Throughout the history of the Jews, stories and legends were passed down from each generation. There were stories of slavery and freedom, sadness and joy, annihilation and redemption. I was obligated to focus on the stories about slavery, sadness and annihilation. I was consumed with fears of our extermination. It engulfed me as it did my father, all year long. Everything and everyone including the Jewish calendar, as explained above, encouraged and enabled me to remember the suffering and atrocities that befell my people.

I remembered our bondage under Pharaoh in Egypt and the barbaric Amalekites in the desert. I remembered the Babylonians and the Romans destroying our Holy Temples and uprooting us from our homeland. I remembered King Antiochus and Haman. I remembered the Spanish Inquisition and the generations of suffrage of our people in Europe by the Crusaders, the English, the Russians, the Poles, the Venetians, the Christian blood libels, the Cossacks, the Moslems and so on. I remember the Holocaust, the massive extermination of one third of our people and my family.

I was taught to dutifully remember it all!

I was committed to these memories, and bound to the feelings of suffrage. I absorbed the pain of hundreds of generations of my people and was committed to pass it along to my children.

Ironically, I remember a well-known Yiddish curse that my father frequently used, "Zol er krenken un gedenken" meaning "Let him suffer and remember."

I had cursed myself! My community cursed themselves! We suffer because we remember. Years of counseling made me realize that my mission in life is not to suffer. My upbringing had left me feeling empty; lacking peace, joy and hope. My foundation was directed by fear. My past led me to fear my present and fear my future.

With all of this resolve, something compelling was clearly missing in our teachings. I have felt a sense of emptiness within me and my Jewish community. There is something we have neglected to understand to help us move spiritually forward as a people to be present and fully connected with God. There is something we have not yet been able to accomplish in all our years of survivability as the children of Israel. There are lessons that we still need to uncover and learn from our oppressive history.

SEVEN

Struggle to Survive

Hear, Israel, the Lord is our God, the Lord is One
In an undertone:
Blessed be the Name of His glorious kingdom
Forever and ever.

You shall love the Lord your God, with all your heart, with all your soul and with all your might. Let these matters that I command you today be upon your heart. Teach them diligently to your children and speak of them while you sit in your home, while you walk on the way, when you retire and when you arise. Bind them as a sign upon your arm and let them be frontlets between your eyes. And write them on the doorposts of your house and upon your gates.

And it will come to pass that if you continually hearken to my commandments that I command you today, to love the Lord your God, and to serve Him, with all your heart and with all your soul -- then I will provide rain for your land in its proper time, the early and late rains, that you may gather in your grain, your wine, and your oil. I will provide grass in your field for your cattle and you will eat and be satisfied. Beware lest your heart be seduced and you turn astray and serve gods of others and bow to them. Then the wrath of God will blaze against you. He will restrain the heaven so there will be no rain and the ground will not yield its produce. And you will swiftly be banished from the goodly land which God gives you.

The Lord spoke to Moses, saying, "Speak to the children of Israel and tell them to make for themselves tzitzit ("fringes") on the corners of their garments throughout their generations, putting a thread of blue upon the corner tzitzit. They will be for you tzitzit, you will see them and be reminded of all the Lord's commandments, and do them, and not turn aside toward your hearts and your eyes and stray after them. So that you remember and do all my commandments and be holy to your God. I am the Lord your God who brought you out of the land of Egypt to be your God; I am the Lord your God. Truth.

- Deuteronomy 6:4

These biblical paragraphs form the most crucial prayer of Judaism, called the "Sh'ma." It is recited twice daily at worship and before one goes to bed. It is the first prayer a Jewish child learns and is the last prayer some Jews will say prior to death.

During World War II, many Jewish children were smuggled into Christian orphanages in various countries to protect them from the Nazis. When the war ended, the Rabbis returned to the orphanages to bring the Jewish children back to surviving family members. As they walked through the corridors where the children slept, the rabbis sang the Sh'ma, and one by one, the Jewish children would come forward from their rooms hoping that their parents were there searching for them.

In first grade, I learned to recite and sing the Sh'ma in Hebrew. This prayer depicts the essence of my Jewish education and my upbringing. Jews are commanded to love God, follow His commandments and teach them diligently to their children.

As a young child, I never quite learned or understood how to love or have a meaningful relationship with God. But I desperately wanted God's love and approval, so I followed the divine commandments as stated in the first paragraph of the Sh'ma. In school each morning during prayers, I would always sit upright, proudly holding my siddur (prayer book), singing and reciting every prayer perfectly in Hebrew. When we finished praying, I closed my siddur, kissed it and carefully placed it back in my desk anticipating the next time I would use it.

When I was nine years old, I went to a neighborhood birthday party and ate a hotdog that tasted funny. When I asked what kind it was, I was told it was an Oscar Meyer hot dog. Immediately, I spit it out of my mouth and into my napkin. I wanted to throw up. God will be angry with me, I thought. I was so ashamed and vowed to never eat non kosher foods again. As I grew, I learned to read the labels and ingredients on food products to determine what foods are permissible to eat. I was afraid of committing sins. Eating dairy and meat products together are also prohibited so I could never eat a cheeseburger or a hamburger with a milkshake. Generally, I waited three hours between eating dairy and meat products because I would not let the food mix and digest together in my body. If I accidentally used a dairy fork with a meat dish in my home, I boiled the utensils and plates in steaming hot water for a couple of hours. I was very careful to follow every law to the fullest degree.

The second paragraph of the Sh'ma is about punishment and reward for obeying or abandoning God's commandments.

As a young teen, I faithfully observed the laws of the Sabbath. From sundown Friday night to sundown Saturday night, I would not drive or ride in a car. I walked everywhere. Touching or sitting on a car would also be considered forbidden since it might lead to driving. Writing, erasing, tearing anything, using electricity and phones were just a few of the prohibitions of the Sabbath. On Friday afternoons before sundown, I ripped sheets of toilet paper and stacked them in the bathroom if there was no tissue in our house; ripping toilet paper was a sin. I checked to insure that the interior refrigerator light was turned off to prevent the light from turning on when I opened the door. Our family used timers to control the rest of the lights and the television in our home but I had no part in such digressions. In biblical times, the punishment for transgressing the Sabbath law was severe. Jews could be stoned to death. I was fearful and not willing to take any chances having God be angry at me.

There are times when the Sabbath laws may be transgressed. As a child, my Rabbis taught me that "Pikuach nefesh" which means saving a life, takes precedence over the Sabbath rules and many other commandments. To question preserving a human life, an obvious moral judgment, versus following the commandments of the Torah demonstrated my Jewish community's fierce adherence and unyielding loyalty to the law.

Being observant made life simple because all the rules were predetermined and laid out just like following the procedures of a manual from start to finish. There was no thinking or understanding. Just as parents instruct their children to follow the mandatory household rules, the children need not understand the significance of the rules but must abide by them or be punished. This was the explanation I received throughout my education in hopes that it would eventually lead me to love God.

The third paragraph of the Sh'ma discusses the "mitzvah" or commandment to wear tzizit, the white fringes which are a physical reminder of observing the 613 commandments in the Torah. This was one of the commandments that is restricted solely to men and thankfully, one less law I had to follow.

As a child of a Holocaust survivor, I felt an additional burden of responsibility to adhere to the commandments. Generations of my family were persecuted and generations of my people were forced into martyrdom because they were Jews. My ancestors in Spain, in the late fifteenth century, were prohibited from practicing their religious beliefs and either forced to convert to Christianity or expelled from their country. Every century following the Spanish Inquisition, Jews throughout Europe were faced with discrimination and oppression.

During World War II, however, Jews were not given the option to convert or be expelled from their countries, they were just murdered. As is now well known, Germans were notoriously fascinated in refining their bloodline to create a pure Aryan race. Labeled as "Eugenics," the Germans' policy began with the elimination of their own mentally retarded population and soon forcefully sterilized hundreds of thousands of their own citizens considered to be defective. The Jews were next in line to be eliminated from society and the Nazis defined "Who is a Jew?" by stating that anyone of Jewish descent, even the descendants of those who converted from Judaism after January 18, 1871, the founding of the German empire, were still considered Jews. The Nuremberg Laws of 1935 were introduced and any citizen descended from three of four Jewish grandparents was defined as a Jew, regardless of whether they practiced or identified as a Jew. Gypsies, homosexuals and other ethnic groups were also subjected to the same treatment as the Jews. The Nazis and their followers murdered my grandmother, aunts, uncles and cousins because they were Jews, and because they could away with it.

Faced with the continuous struggles to survive as a people, Jews have always attempted to follow their rich traditions and laws striving to connect with God. I think of this covenant as a connective cord binding and uniting one generation to the next and carrying along the religious teachings. I also consider it like a fetus connected by the umbilical cord to receive the nourishment and oxygen from the mother to survive.

I was not going to be the one to cut the cord of my lineage and break the covenant of my people. Like my father, I felt it was important that I live in a Jewish neighborhood surrounded by synagogues, Jewish schools, shops and Jewish neighbors so that I could raise my family the proper way.

Emil Fackenheim, a noted Jewish philosopher and Holocaust survivor, once said that a 614th commandment needs to be inserted into Jewish law. He remarked, "Thou shalt not hand Hitler posthumous victories. To despair of the God of Israel is to continue Hitler's work for him."

Fackenheim realized that in order to oppose Hitler's goals of eliminating the Jewish people, Jews must observe their faith.

I think that just as the traditions and laws of Judaism linked one generation to the next, the devastating effects of generations of persecution and anti-Semitism bonded us as a people and unnoticeably molded and solidified our thoughts, feelings and behaviors into a collective consciousness. The teachings that I have learned were influenced by traumatic events in Jewish history.

Fear of extinction is one of the devastating effects of anti-Semitism. It has haunted us as a people from generation to generation. Fear that the world around us will attempt to eradicate us seeped into our minds and shaped a victim-like mentality. It created an imprint of terror, darkness and suffering which have become part of our identity as a people and has directed our lives and created our destiny.

The connective cord of my lineage carries this deeply embedded fear which often goes unnoticed, yet it has influenced us as a people and continues to innately be a part of us today.

We cling to this fear of annihilation just as our ancestors did and we unconsciously pass it along to our children. I believe that fear creates dysfunction among ourselves. It keeps us from being whole and spiritually connected to each other and to God.

Vowing to never forget the plight of my people and compelled to insure their tormented past remain alive and present within me, I unknowingly carried the pangs of all this negativity.

Bound to this inseparable and invisible cord, it tangled, attached and settled itself to my innermost being. My mind, body and spirit were all influenced by these thought forms.

I was unaware how these thoughts influenced my life. This invisible effect consumed my thoughts, played havoc with my emotions and distorted my reality. Unknowingly, I was imprisoned by this fear of annihilation.

When I became pregnant for the first time, thoughts of my people's survival emerged and I was overcome by sadness, anger and resentment against the world. The mere thought of telling my children that they are hated because they carry the bloodline of their ancestors would be excruciatingly unjust. Even though my life was relatively free of anti-Semitism, I wanted them to know that the world is prejudiced against them simply because they are Jews. They had to learn that they will always need to watch their backs throughout their lives. I vowed to make sure of that.

There is yet another form of fear of extermination that exists within segments of our people. It is the fear of assimilation. In my family, the thought of marrying a non-Jew was sacrilegious. God forbid, if I'd even considered dating a non-Jew, my father would have thrown me out of the house.

Wherever we have wandered throughout our history, many communities have been afraid of succumbing to the attractive and tempting lifestyle of the non-Jew. In fact, a percentage of Jews had always assimilated and intermarried with their neighbors. When I was a college student, I lived in the dormitory at the University of Illinois in Chicago. One night a group of students from our dorm floor planned to go dancing in the city. However, Jeff, a non-Jewish student, and I were the only ones available so we grabbed dinner downtown and went dancing on Rush Street. When we returned to the dormitory, he walked me back to my room. Surprisingly, he turned to me, held my hands and kissed me on the cheek. I remained standing aghast in the hallway. I wiped my cheek, cried and felt like a traitor.

With one-third of our population murdered in the Holocaust, many Jews are fearful that we will lose more Jews to assimilation and intermarriage, which will further cause the deterioration of our people. Our survival is at stake.

Marrying outside the faith carries different penalties in many Jewish communities. In some families it would be considered a death and the married couple would be excommunicated from the family and community. In other communities, the couple would be shunned. There are some families that would expect the non-Jew to convert to Judaism with the promise of raising the children Jewish, while other sects of Judaism will accept one Jewish parent as long as they raise the children Jewish. In biblical times, patrilineal descent determined the Jewish bloodline of the child; however, today some movements of Judaism consider a Jew only through matrilineal descent while other movements would consider patrilineal descent and not all Jewish sects consider all conversions legitimate. Jewish genetic purity continues to be questioned within the Jewish community, as it was by Hitler, and the question continues "Who is a Jew?".

This fear of assimilation that was instilled in my upbringing made me very critical of my fellow Jews. I learned that my religious practices were the key to the survival of my people and the only true path to connect with God. I became highly judgmental toward any Jew who did not observe Judaism to the same strict degree the way I practiced my faith. I knew and understood the exact tenets and desires of God. My Jewish community taught me that the world is a seductive and enticing place and I could easily assimilate and eventually intermarry. Therefore, our laws bind us together as a people distinguishing us from our neighbors. Our survival depends how we live day to day separating ourselves from the culture of the non-Jew. My family kept kosher and drank only kosher wines to prevent us from socializing with the non-Jew. The 613 commandments help us survive as a unique and distinctive people, and protect us from assimilation.

Interestingly, we created a very precarious and paralyzing situation for our people. On one hand, there is the fear that our surrounding neighbors will harm or kill us and yet if they welcome and accept us, there is the fear of assimilation and intermarriage. We cannot win either way. I feel that many people in my Jewish community are stuck in this duality, which creates a place of mental havoc and cripples us internally.

For hundreds of generations, Jewish communities have struggled with this dichotomy. These fears continue to mold, manipulate and direct many of our communities today. My Orthodox community was bound and committed to these fears and welcomed them with open arms. There are times in our history when danger is ever present and our fears are legitimate. But many in my community today live as if we are in constant peril.

Can we liberate ourselves from the fears of both acceptance and losing our unique identity with too much acceptance? How do we connect with our neighbors but insure that our connection with Judaism remains intact and secure? How can we live at peace?

As a people, we have lived with these fears and will die with these fears. We have passed them along to the next generation and they too are marked by these fears.

In 1990, during my second pregnancy, I discovered that I was carrying an abnormal fetus. Prior to my abortion, I fell into my mother's arms sobbing and said, "Don't worry about me, Mom, as devastating as this appears, I will survive this ordeal. After all, this is not as tragic as the Holocaust. I will bring more children into this world."

I cried with my mother and only with her. I never talked or shared my trauma with anyone again. Carrying all the anger and sadness inside of me was my way of coping with life. Besides, talking or complaining about my sorrows and difficulties seemed trivial and insignificant. How could I? They seemed irrelevant compared with the suffering my father and my people endured. My loyalty remained to my father, my ancestors and my people. They endured the suffering so that I would survive. They sacrificed their lives so that I can be here today to continue on with the lineage of my family and people. My loyalty was my gift of appreciation to my ancestors. Their affliction would not be in vain.

Nor would I listen to anyone else kvetch about their lives. After my abortion, when an old friend complained about her queasiness during her first trimester of pregnancy, I walked out of the room. I also refused to answer questions about losing a fetus and wouldn't let anyone call it a child.

I knew I wasn't myself, but had no idea how to change. My husband's response to a seldom complaint was to hush me up. It was just five months after my mother died and I was still grieving and crying. My husband said to me, "Get over it already. It is time to move on."

So I basically stopped talking to him and never shared any of my sadness with anyone else. I realize I was enslaved to the phantoms of my past. The fear seduced me and I was bonded by these painful memories. It was an incestuous link that was not protecting me or healing me. I ultimately was disloyal and irreverent to myself, my family and my people.

When my brother, Howard, died at thirty-five-years old, I fumed at God! How cruel for God to take another young Jewish life! My brother was an Orthodox pulpit rabbi. How could he die? Why would God let another innocent Jewish life pass? Were there not enough victims from our family in the Holocaust? Could God not spare my brother? He was a kind and charitable man. He was a loving son, husband, father, brother and respectable community leader. How much pain does my mother need to endure? Did my father not suffer enough in his life by witnessing the murder of his family and then burying his first-born son? Why did my brother Barry and I need to lose our big brother? Why was God cursing my family? I faithfully followed all the laws of my people, so why was God punishing me? I had no answers, but this anger congealed and planted its roots within me. For several years following my brother's death, I remained angry and bitter toward God. Eventually, the bitterness dissipated and turned into sadness. I wasn't interested in seeing plays, movies or listening to music on the radio. I did my best to bring some enjoyment into my mother's life by having her spend as much time as possible with my children. My life continued on habitually following the laws of the Torah and busy raising a family. Again I suffered in silence.

I was fearful, uncertain and unaware if my niece and nephew were going to be raised properly Jewish since our entire family was cut off from their lives. Barry was single and the burden of responsibility to carry on my family lineage and heritage was on my shoulders. Beginning at three years old, my children began their religious training in a Jewish preschool. I schlepped them to synagogue each Shabbat and every Jewish holiday so they could begin learning the traditions and prayers of the services. Eventually, my children would be old enough to learn the Sh'ma with all their heart, with all their soul and with all their might, exactly the way I did.

Recently I attended a prayer class during which the Rabbi explained the historical origins of the Sh'ma. The three paragraphs of this prayer were inserted into the daily prayers and replaced the Ten Commandments in the first century A.D. The early Christians, who were Jews, believed that it was not necessary to abide by all the 613 laws of the Torah; the Ten Commandments sufficed.

Fearful of the early Christians attempt to dilute and alter the current Jewish practices of that time, and wanting to protect the survivorship of the Jewish people, our rabbis clearly maintained that Jews were obligated to follow all the commandments of the Torah. By removing the Ten Commandments from the daily prayers, they distinguished themselves from the early Christian philosophy and encouraged Jews to follow all the laws of the Torah.

During the Holocaust my father was fortunate to befriend one Christian family in Hamburg, and they ultimately saved his life during the war. They hid him and gave him food and clothes until he was strong enough to move on. Without the aid of this Christian family, he may have perished.

There are over 22,000 non-Jews who have been honored by Israel and recognized at Yad Vashem, the Holocaust Memorial in Jerusalem. They are designated as "The Righteous among the Nations" and have rescued Jews by hiding them, providing false documents and identities and smuggling them into safer locations and countries. They were Christians and Moslems, educated professionals and illiterate farmers, religious and non-religious citizens from over forty-four countries.

The rabbis who perceived the early Christians as distorting the ancient ways of life would have been surprised to see that their offspring had eventually helped save Jews during the Holocaust.

Fear of the extermination of our people was the motive for inserting these biblical passages called the Sh'ma into our daily prayers. Fear that Jews will veer away from God and our survival will again be at stake is the underlying theme coursing through the Sh'ma. Many may not consider this idea as truth and choose to negate it or suggest this prayer is a metaphor and not to be taken literally. Then I wonder which prayers, words and commandments of the Torah is a figure of speech and which are meant literally?

Some may consider that there are advantages to instilling fear in our people. It can be a powerful teaching tool and motivator for our youth and the entire Jewish community to keep us tightly bound as a unique and distinctive people from generation to generation. Are there any negative repercussions to this teaching method? Is there possibly another way to instill the beauty of Judaism into the lives of the youth without using fear tactics? Can we let go of the fear and still remain loyal to our people?

My rabbi also shared a very beautiful and most interesting third century "midrash" or folk tale regarding the first two lines of the Sh'ma. When Jacob our patriarch, who later became known as Israel, was lying on his death bed, he reflected back on his past and pondered his future generations. He thought about his grandfather Abraham, who had two children, Ishmael and Isaac, who became patriarchs to two separate nations. Isaac continued following the path of the Hebrews while Ishmael became the father to the nation of Arabs. Jacob and Esau, twins to Isaac and Rebecca also took different paths and just like Isaac, Jacob followed his father's path while Esau left the Hebrews to father another Semitic nation. Jacob (Israel) was noticeably concerned about this familial pattern and the future of his seed. He wondered if his children will remain united and follow the ways of the Hebrews or veer off to another path. His children surrounded him at his death bed and said,

"Hear O Israel, the Lord is our God, the Lord is One".

Then silently, Jacob (Israel) responded: Blessed be the Name of His glorious kingdom forever and ever.

When I imagine myself on my death bed, I might see my whole life flash before my eyes. It may begin with my recollection of early childhood memories and end with my final years of life. I may think about my family, friends and enemies and how I related to each one of them. I may ponder over fond memories and difficult experiences I endured. I may think about whom I loved and who I hurt. I may contemplate my accomplishments and my failures and think about my future generations.

Jacob's life was full of so many trials and tribulations but the rabbis focused on one particular, possible scenario of Jacob's last thoughts on his death bed, the struggle to survive. The rabbis of the third century effectively demonstrated their own reflections of themselves on their death bed. The fear of extinction for the Jewish people would remain ingrained in them until their own demise.

This fear of annihilation had dominated my existence. I felt spiritually depleted. Letting go of these fears seemed to be the answer to creating a more harmonious and loving way of life.

EIGHT

Do the Right Thing

Do what you feel in your heart to be right—for you'll be criticized anyway.
~ Eleanor Roosevelt

The hospital room was quite small and cramped with several people huddling near my father. The curtain that split the room in half was drawn to create a sense of privacy on my father's side. Beba leaned over the foot of his bed, attempting to understand the conversation. Sitting at my father's right side was the social worker wearing her crisp, white hospital lab coat holding a clipboard with several forms and a pen in hand. I was standing to the left side of the bed waiting for my father to reach a conclusion.

It was spring of 2003; my father was hospitalized with a urinary tract infection that caused him to be confused and delusional. Deeply concerned about his physical and mental wellbeing, when my father returned to his normal state of mind, I explained to him the urgency of appointing someone to be his medical power of attorney.

"Daddy," I reiterated, "you were unconscious for a day from your infection. You need to decide who you want to act as your medical power of attorney. Do you want Barry, Beba or me?"

My father did not respond. The social worker brought the necessary documents to my dad's hospital room. She moved closer to my father's side since I mentioned to her that he was hard of hearing and she proceeded to speak in a loud voice, "Mr. Kaplan, I am the hospital social worker. I have the papers ready for you to sign. Have you made a decision?"

My father's eyebrows lowered, wrinkles appeared in his forehead, and his face cringed. He propped himself up in his hospital bed, flung his arms and yelled, "Take the papers avay, I vill not sign them!"

He glared and pointed his finger right at me and then turned to the social worker. He continued, "You see this voman standing over my bed, she murdered my vife!"

My eyes popped open and I froze for a moment before turning to the social worker and saying, "I don't think my father is ready to make any decisions today, please come back another time."

How absurd and downright stupid for my father to accuse me of killing my own mother! It was the first and only time he ever said anything like that. He caught me off guard; it was so farfetched and shocking that I couldn't believe I heard the words emanating from his mouth. It was so unexpected. Or was it?

During the summer of 1997, when my mother was hospitalized with terminal cancer, she appointed me to be her medical power of attorney. She knew that I would be the one to respect her dying wishes. Barry was too emotionally fragile to make any decisions and my father came by just a few times a week. Toward the end of her life, she was in an insurmountable amount of pain and just wanted to die quickly. I advocated for her and fought to provide her with an ample amount of morphine so that she died peacefully with dignity.

My father, however, had an entirely different perspective on life and death. He learned to coexist with pain and suffering while surviving during the war. He had learned to cling to life, at all costs. He never gave up, not even to the day he died. Quality of life had no bearing on his views; he was a survivor. Although I honored my mother's wishes, he firmly believed that I encouraged her death and even murdered her.

There was also another reason why my father reacted so strongly. Rightfully paranoid of everyone during the war, he would have been in a dangerous situation, if not deadly one, if he placed trust in anyone. So he learned to depend only on himself alone and control his own fate. His life was in his hands. After the war, no one was to be trusted, not even his wife or children. He could not conceive of relinquishing control and transferring authority over his life; therefore, he was adamant about not signing the papers. He felt as if he was losing control and became terrified and angry, directing his wrath at me.

The last weekend in November 2007, I met a friend downtown. As we waited for the light to turn green at the corner of Dearborn and Ontario, a huge bird flew toward me and swooped over my head. When I turned around, it attacked a pigeon standing in the crevice of the Excalibur (a Romanesque Revival designed building which is now a nightclub) wall just five feet behind me.

"That was a hawk!" my friend said.

"Wow! That bird flew just a few inches over your head," remarked a passer-by.

"I didn't know that hawks live in downtown Chicago," I said.

"They don't. I have never seen one in all my years living in this part of the city," said my friend.

As I witnessed the hawk kill the pigeon, I cringed with disgust. Both birds were shrieking and it looked barbaric. We walked across the street, picked up some Starbucks coffee and retrieved the car. I looked over and saw the hawk standing with its wings spanning wide open, bobbing its head and devouring its prey.

During the weekend I thought about this strange occurrence and sent my cousin Alisha this email. Alisha and I are both granddaughters of Max. She is the granddaughter from his first wife while I am the granddaughter from his second marriage to my Bubbie Rae. Our mothers were half-sisters who spoke to each other every day. After my mother died, Alisha became the sister I always wanted; in fact many people think we are sisters. She is fifteen years older than me and very loving and protective toward my family and me. Yet sometimes the roles reverse and I feel like I am her older sister offering her welcomed advice. Alisha, too, is a first-generation American, as both sides of her family immigrated to America during the early 1900s. Her father fled Eastern Europe escaping the pogroms and the Russian army at age 15, while her mother was born on the ship on route to America. I always looked up to Alisha; she finished high school early and graduated college with a double major in three years. At 23 years and pregnant with her second child, she received her Master's in Math Education. She has A.D.D. and often bounces from topic to topic in our daily conversations; yet when I need her help, she tunes in clearly and is present for me. Alisha cannot tolerate crowds and feels insecure around people she doesn't know. She has told me that in the entire world, one of her favorite places to be is with me and my children because she feels calm and safe with us. I know that she comes from an abusive household and noticed over the years that she has a survivor mentality. She will be the first one to sit down to eat and make sure she has enough food on her plate. Alisha has a heart of gold and is always bringing gifts and trinkets over to us. Alisha and I count our blessings that we have each other in our lives.

November 2007
Hi Alisha,

As I was driving home from the city, I began to wonder about the meaning of this odd occurrence. While I was meditating, this is what came to me. The hawk and pigeon are an omen of my future. It was necessary for me to witness the hawk strike and kill the pigeon as well as feed on it. At first I thought this entire incident was violent and revolting. But then I realized the hawk kills not for the sport but to survive and was forced to fly out of its natural environment into the city to find food. The time will come when I need to take a stance. It will not be for the sake of greed but for the sake of my future. It may appear unethical or distasteful, but it is a necessary move. So as bad as it will look (like the hawk killing the pigeon) it is vital to my existence and the security of my family.

When the time comes, remind me when I start to feel scared or when I think I may be acting unethical and deceitful that I need to be the hawk; the one who takes control for the purpose of security, survival and life.

Love,
Karen :)

Little did I know that when I wrote this email to Alisha, my future would parallel this story.

Strange Insight

On a whim, in the summer of 2008, I went with a group of girl-friends for a fun night out to see a well-known psychic who had a reputation for providing incredible details and insight into the future. In my private session with her, she immediately began to describe a biblical story of a blind, old man who was married with two sons.

"There was a familial discord over a birthright and inheritance," she said, "I am not too familiar with the entire story."

"You are referring to the Jewish patriarch, Isaac, who became blind as an old man and was married to Rebecca. They had twin sons Esau and Jacob," I said.

"Go on and tell me more," she said.

"The Torah explains that Rebecca and her son Jacob coerced and plotted to steal the inheritance from Esau, the elder twin. After Jacob received Isaac's blessing and the birthright, he fled his home to escape his brother's wrath. Esau was angered and planned to kill Jacob," I added.

The psychic nodded and said, "Now I understand the message I received."

"What is the relevance of this story to my life?" I asked.

"Karen, you need to be concerned about a destructive decision your father made in his will. As a result of his decision, your brother and you may become estranged from one another," she said.

"What are you talking about?" I asked surprisingly.

"You must act gingerly," she warned me.

"Act gingerly?" I repeated. "No, I think you are mistaken. This is not fathomable." I continued. "As a matter of fact, over the years I asked my father and brother if they ever updated the will after my mother died and was told nothing was ever done."

The psychic seems unbothered by my curt response and firmly repeated, "Act with caution."

She then proceeded with the rest of my reading, but I could not focus on anything else she said. My mind kept on reverting back to her warnings and the will.

When I returned home, immediately I raced into my office and searched the file cabinet for the copy of my parents' will. My parents had updated it after Howard passed away in 1991. After rereading the contents of the will, I felt somewhat relieved. However, as days passed, I felt a gnawing inside of me; my stomach was tightening into knots and I was jittery. I could not shake off these feelings. So I drove into the city to my father's condo and walked directly to his file cabinets stationed in the corner of the dining room. I searched through his files and found the folder that contained the wills. As I opened the folder, I saw the exact copy which I retained in my home. It said that upon the death of both parents, Barry would be appointed executor and the estate would be equally divided between the two of us. A small amount of the inheritance was also bequeathed to my three children.

Then I was astonished to find that my father had another will updated in 2005! It stated that upon the death of my father, my brother once again was appointed executor of the will and my children were to receive a similar amount of inheritance. However, it also said that my brother would inherit 99 percent of the estate and I was bequeathed less than one percent and only upon the following conditions.

The above heir must be committed to a Jewish lifestyle and not marry outside the Jewish faith. Karen should not request any additional funds for either her or her children from Barry beyond what is designated in the will.

I reread these words one more time thinking that I misunderstood the contents; but it was there in black and white! My jaw dropped and I felt a huge pit in my stomach. Shocked at my discovery, all I could do was stand in the middle of the dining room paralyzed. This was incomprehensible, I thought. Why did they lie to me? Eventually, I called Alisha and read her the will.

"What do I do, Alisha?" I asked.

"Karen", she said, "all you need to do now is to make a copy of the will and return the original back into the file. Then go home and we can talk about it later on. You are in shock."

As the days followed, I reread this will over and over. I barely ate and had a hard time falling asleep. One afternoon as I was driving, I thought I slowed down to brake with the traffic. Instead, my head fell forward in a slump and I fell asleep behind the wheel. I crashed into the car in front of me. Luckily I wasn't hurt and neither were the passengers in the next two cars ahead of me that were also impacted.

A repugnant feeling permeated my entire body penetrating to my core. It was as if someone just jammed a knife into my heart and pulled it right out. Why would my own father and brother deceive me? What did I ever do to them to deserve this? They are all I have left of my nuclear family. My father also planned in advance that I couldn't get additional money from my brother no matter what. What chutzpah! I was divorced, raising three children and trying to make ends meet, while my brother was single and wealthy. I never expected more than my fair share, if and when the time came.

Why did Barry hide the will from me? I thought he loved me and cared for me. I thought we looked out for each other. Our family went through so much pain and hurt, why would he cause me more? My anger began to congeal. I prayed for help because without it I would resort to cutting off all ties with my brother and father and never speaking to either one of them again. That was my typical pattern. Anyone who had dared wrong me morally or ethically was immediately cast out of my life; I never just fired friends indiscriminately.

"Mommy," I prayed to myself, "Barry and Daddy have betrayed me. What do I do? How do I move forward? How do I ever look Barry in the eye, let alone keep him in my life? I know in my heart that you would want Barry and me to get along. Please help me."

What was I supposed to do? How do I proceed from here? Do I talk to my father and brother about the will? Absolutely not! I knew I would gain nothing by confronting either Barry or my father. I have learned from my father's character that a liar will always be a liar, and when confronted and cornered, a liar will do what a liar does best. Lie!

It was already the end of September 2008, and a few months had passed since I discovered the will. Still feeling helpless, I called a friend in California, David, who also knew my brother. David had worked for Barry for a few years and understood Barry's character. David was also extremely intuitive.

"Karen, get your brother to take your father back to the attorney and have the will changed," he suggested.

"How do you propose I suggest this to my brother?" I asked sarcastically.

"Here is the plan and follow it exactly," he said with confidence as he began to construct an absolutely ridiculous scenario.

I listened with growing misgivings, but since high school I'd known David to be someone of incredible perception and prescience. Still I was baffled. "Are you kidding me? Is this some kind of a joke? I can't fabricate a nightmare. I can't pretend to be Tevye from *Fiddler on the Roof* and pull off this stunt!"

David said, "Listen to me. I am positive that this is the right thing to do. Do it!"

So the next morning, I called Barry and began to describe my fabricated nightmare with all the drama I could muster.

"Barry," I began, "last night I had the most God awful, scary dream."

"What was it about?" he asked.

"Mommy and Howard were there; she was crying hysterically and Howard was screaming."

"Why?" asked Barry.

I thought I hooked him already. I lowered my voice to a whisper, "They were repeating these words, Do the right thing! Do the right thing!"

"Go on," said Barry.

"They were not directing these words at me, Barry. Mommy was so miserable and just kept on crying. She kept on telling me that you need to do the right thing. Then Howard, as he was standing on a large pulpit wearing his kippah and tallit (prayer shawl), said: 'there will be consequences if Barry does not do the right thing.' He was upset."

I kept at it for a while making up details about how our mom and brother looked, adding a few threats.

Over the years, Barry mentioned to me that he believed Howard was watching over him from the spiritual world; he thought Howard was his guardian angel helping him with his overall success in business and financial matters. Knowing this made it easier for me to sell Barry this lie. I hated to be devious but I had no other plan in place. How was I going to get my brother to admit what he had done? Besides, the financial security of my family was at stake and I needed to take responsibility for my children.

Barry was noticeably quiet on the other end of the line.

He finally spoke, "Are you sure that is exactly what they said?"

"Yes," I replied, wanting at this point to get off the phone.

"What do you think they meant by 'do the right thing'?" he asked nervously.

I added a breathing tremor to my answer, "I don't know....what do you think it means?"

He sighed, "I cleaned up all my business affairs with my accountant this past year. Everything is all legal. I don't understand what they could possibly mean?"

I answered slowly, "Barry, please figure this one out. It was painful watching Mommy crying and Howard so angry; it nearly broke my heart."

By now I detected fear in my brother's voice. Again he asked me what I thought they meant in the dream.

Early the next morning he called me back and asked me to repeat the dream. Ugh, I thought to myself. I hate doing this and I hate all these lies. But there was no other option. So I repeated this entire fabrication, trying to get everything right a second time. When I finished, he sounded like a ghost himself, and I think he might have been crying. Nothing appeared to materialize from our conversation, as the weeks passed. Something else needed to be done, I thought, but I had no other ideas.

Then in early October, Barry turned 50 and I turned 46.

That year he sent me a birthday card that I still remember to this day. On the cover was an older woman who said "There is only one thing you can do to avoid old age." On the inside of the card, in large bold letters it read, "Lie!". How appropriate I thought. He just confirmed what I believe he was doing all these years; lying to me.

Barry flew in for Thanksgiving and stayed at his lavish three-bedroom, high-rise condo with a gorgeous view of Lake Michigan and the Chicago Loop, which he uses only during his infrequent, short summer and fall visits. My children and I celebrated his birthday Saturday night by taking him out to Maggiano's in Skokie and buying him a beautiful handmade wooden desk set. I also invited my cousin Alisha to dinner; she acted as my buffer, just in case.

Later that evening he called me up and said, "I was hoping that you would have thrown a party for me."

But all I could manage to say was "Throw you a party?", my jaws clenched. "You hardly have any friends living here and you rarely speak to any of our relatives. Who did you want me to invite?"

Barry was angry at first and repeated that he'd hoped for a party. Then he sighed and sounded kind of defeated. "This is a special year for me, I thought you might want to do something more than take me out for dinner and buy me a gift."

"If there were people to invite, I might have considered it," I responded, as gently as I could while biting my tongue and clenching my fists (and to myself I added he has a lot of audacity to ask me to do anything for him).

Barry stayed in Chicago for the entire weekend and said that he would return in the spring to help our father with his tax returns.

A Plan in Place

My father depended on me more frequently as his health continued to deteriorate. I drove him the dentist to repair and clean his dentures and saw the audiologist at Costco to fix his hearing aids and pick up free batteries. He scheduled appointments with his internist, urologist and psychiatrist and always asked for free samples of medication at their offices; many times we went there just to pick up the free samples. I took him shopping for groceries and renewed all his bank CDs (scattered throughout the city and suburbs) the day they matured. I checked his mail, paid his bills, filed his bank statements in the dining room cabinets and took him to the Jewish Community Center to pick up the Jewish newspapers.

We schlepped everywhere. I also needed to attend the monthly meetings at his condo unit and met with roofing and tuck pointing contractors and service repair workers at his building. There were multiple times during those years when he was hospitalized, sometimes for weeks, and driving daily back and forth to the hospital in the city was overwhelming. There were many days when I couldn't even get home in time to pick up my children from school or make them dinner. I was torn between taking care of my father and taking care of my children, but aside from Beba, I was all he had. Thankfully, Beba washed his clothes, fed him, gave him his medication and took care of him in the evenings.

Oddly, my brother was no longer visiting consistently, so most of the responsibility for his care fell on my shoulders.

I was exhausted and still was not sleeping very well since the car accident; I worried incessantly about taking care of my family. I was cobbling together part-time work that allowed me to still take care of my children full time. My child support and maintenance payments did not cover all my personal expenses like car, health insurance and dental bills.

Then one day when I was heading over to my father's, I suddenly remembered what happened when Howard died. He inadvertently left my parents' name on one of his bank CDs; most likely, he forgot to replace my parents' names with Helene's name after his wedding. Helene called my parents and said, "I have sent you a copy of Howard's and my will. As you can see, he left everything to me. So you will need to relinquish the money from the bank CD that has your names on it and forward all the money to me."

My father responded, "I vill give you the money on vone condition. You must send the children to Jewish Day School. My son vould have vanted them to be raised in a private school. Send me the bill and I vill pay the tuition from the account."

"Don't tell me what to do with my money. Give it all to me," she demanded.

"I vill not," my father replied.

"Then I will sue you for it," yelled Helene.

"Go ahead!" he said and added his usual Yiddish curses when he hung up.

Helene sued my father and she lost. We also lost. It has been over twenty years since I've seen Howard's children. This family misfortune, however, was the key to answering my prayers about how I would raise my family as a single parent. I realized that the will had no bearing on my father's bank accounts and stocks. All I had to do was insure that my name would appear on every CD and stock as a co-owner. This was going to take some time and effort to accomplish.

As I continued helping my father each week, I started paying closer attention to his bank statements and all his financial records. I discovered that Barry's name appeared on all the accounts and stocks as a co-owner. My name had been either deleted or it was followed by the initials P.O.D.

(payable upon death). This meant that my brother would become the sole owner of everything after my father's death. I would be Barry's beneficiary. I was so hurt that they had plotted against me in this way; I started to ache all over and couldn't stop crying.

After crying myself out, I sat up in bed and realized that I had to do something. I created a chart on my laptop listing all the banks, their addresses, accounts, ownership of the accounts, dates of maturity and a detailed list of the stocks and bonds. In fact, I showed my father this list so he could see when all these CDs were maturing. The stock certificates, however, were locked away in a safety deposit box at a bank in West Rogers Park to which only my father and Barry had access.

One day a few weeks later, after I'd calmed down and thought more clearly, I was driving my father to one of his banks. I passed the bank statement to him and asked with only a slight tremor in my voice, if there was a reason why my name was not included on the account. Then I asked him if he would like to add my name to all of his accounts. I had a tape recorder with me and managed to press the button to record our conversation. He responded that he wanted my name on the accounts, which was kind of surprising, but then he didn't say anything else. Why was he amendable to my request? I couldn't believe that he changed his mind. That was very strange, I thought, and wondered why he deleted my name in the first place? I had no answers.

A week later, he asked me for the first time to research banks. I felt like maybe he had started to trust me more, and happily did my homework. I was delighted to give him information on which banks offered the highest rates. (Amusingly, my friends were impressed with my knowledge and soon began asking me for advice on where to deposit their own money.)

Once a CD matured (and this was a lot of driving because he had over thirty bank accounts), I drove my father to the bank and we asked the bankers to match the top rates of that week. If they wouldn't, we withdrew the money and deposited it elsewhere. Although it wasn't everything he had, I thought it was a tremendous amount of money, and realized that if my name wasn't on the account, Barry would have taken all of it. I was struggling, he was comfortable, and although I knew that what I did next was sneaky, I felt like I had to do it for my children's future. I added my name onto every account alongside my father's name whenever possible and told the banker to delete or add P.O.D. to Barry's name. My goal was to make everything equitable between Barry and me. Changing the ownership of the stocks was more difficult; Barry's signature would be needed to make the changes. So I decided to focus all my energy on the bank accounts.

That wasn't even the worst of my behavior and I know you are sitting in judgment as you read this, but please hear me out. Several CDs were not going to mature for a few years and I wanted to add my name to them as well. My only option was to break the CDs and incur penalties. That was a small price to pay insuring that Barry and I would equally share the inheritance, I thought. My father would have never agreed to break a CD and lose money, but he never knew what was really going on. Anyway, I decided that I would offer to pay any penalties. So while we sat with the bankers, I was squirming and sweating, as we both told them that my name was to be added to all the accounts. Since his hearing progressively became worse, he didn't know that we were actually breaking the CDs.

Alisha and I would chat daily and I said to her one morning, "The dream I fabricated was not that far from the truth. Both my mother and Howard would be devastated knowing that Barry had plotted with my father against me. In fact, before my mother died, while she was lying in the hospital bed, she wrote me a check and depleted her savings. (Later on in her life, she finally stood up against my father by keeping her own money. I never realized how courageous this must have been and I wished I could have told her how proud I was of her.) She knew that Barry was doing financially well and that I could use a few extra dollars for my children. She always put her children and grandchildren before her own needs."

Alisha said, "I know your mom would be disappointed in Barry. She suffered all those years living with your father and having very little money. She would be turning over in her grave knowing that you were cut out of the will. You absolutely have to secure your future for your family. I know you're feeling deceitful, but you really did do the right thing." She also pointed out that everything seemed to be going my way; she suggested patience, and she was right.

The next week, my father, out of the blue, asked me to take him to his safety box to review all his stocks. This was ridiculously unbelievable. He had never before asked me to take him there. We drove over to the bank in West Rogers Park. We went downstairs to the lowest level, signed in with the guard and entered the secured room (I also signed forms permitting me access to the box at any time). It was as if I was having a day when all my prayers were answered.

My father carried his deposit box key on his key chain and I didn't know if Barry had the second key. We unlocked the box and I found all of his stock certificates folded neatly inside. There were also his immigration papers from the time he left Germany as well as some genealogy records. I grabbed the certificates and told my father that I would review them and return them another time. We left the bank and I drove him back to Beba's place.

I was dumbfounded. So I called Alisha and told her everything that just transpired. Even though I was not stealing from my father, I felt deceitful about not being completely upfront about breaking the CDs. Then I told Alisha a story that I recalled as a child in my home. Every Saturday morning my father would go to "shul" (synagogue) and my brothers and I would notice my mother sneaking into his bedroom closet and taking money out of his wallet. It appeared that my mother was stealing from him. As I grew into adulthood, I realized that my mother each week handed over her payroll check to my father. She needed money for the household and was tired of begging for money and fighting with him. So she averted additional havoc and chaos by taking money while he was praying in the synagogue. She handled the situation the best way she knew how and I always had a lot of respect for my mother.

A month after my trip to the safety deposit box, in March 2009, my brother came back into town to help my father with his annual tax returns as he always did. Barry along with my two younger children, Noah and Raquel, went out to dinner at R.J. Grunts in Lincoln Park near his apartment. He asked me, "Karen, do you know anything about broken CDs from the banks? I have spent the last two days with the accountant and bankers trying to figure all this out. This is very troubling. Daddy would never break a CD and lose money. This doesn't make any sense."

I felt my heart pounding. It never occurred to me that the banks would report the penalties. What was I thinking? I knew I was nailed. Damn, I thought. What do I do now? I couldn't respond, not there in front of my children; I needed some time to figure out what to do. So I lied and said, "No, I don't know."

Then my stomach just dropped. I felt I was on a roller coaster spiraling downward. So I excused myself from the table, lurched to the restroom and called Alisha. She heard me heaving and asked, "Karen, what's wrong?"

"I'm scared. Barry knows about the broken CDs. It is just a matter of days that he will discover what I have been doing this past year. He'll tell my father. My children and I will lose everything."

"Karen, stay calm. You will pull through. Call me when you all get home. Don't say or do anything now."

Alisha never let me down. She was always there for me when I needed her.

So I returned to the table, trying to maintain my composure. I couldn't put a drop of food or drink in my body. I sat there anxiously waiting for everyone to finish their meals. We said our goodbyes and walked back to our cars. While driving home, I noticed that my hands were trembling and turning clammy as I grasped the steering wheel tightly. My mind began racing and thoughts about the security and future of my family became dismal. I knew that once Barry told my father what I had done, they would cut me out of their lives.

Noah and Raquel dozed off while we were driving home on the highway and I began talking to my mother and brother in spirit. "What do I do now? It is a matter of days until they will know everything," I mumbled to myself.

At that moment, along the highway, my attention veered to a license plate that displayed two letters "HK", both my mother's and brother's initials. I looked at it and said to myself, "What are you both trying to tell me?" As I quickly drove pass that car, I noticed the next license plate read "KOL TOV" a Hebrew expression that means "everything is good". So I said to my mom and brother, "How could everything be good? This entire family is falling apart. I have been betrayed!"

I pulled into my driveway, dropped off my children and told them I would be right back. Within one second after they exited the car, I had shortness of breath. My heart began pounding and my entire body was trembling. I started hyperventilating. I felt so scared and all alone. I started to wonder if I did the right thing all along. Driving aimlessly on the dark side streets of Deerfield, I began to cry. Then I remembered to call my cousin. I explained to her what happened on the highway driving home; from HK to Kol Tov.

Alisha asked, "Are you driving the car?"

"Yes," I said.

"Well pull over, stop the car and take some deeps breaths. You will get through this just fine. Listen to the message your mother and brother just sent you," she asserted.

So I pulled over and my lights beamed at a lawn sign which read, "Harriet is running for Mayor of Deerfield." Was this another sign from my mother? I disregarded it. Alisha stayed on the phone with me until my breathing returned to normal. Then I drove home and was restless all night.

It was early in the morning and I had barely slept. I went to the health club to work out but I could not concentrate and had very little energy. So I sat at the food bar and called my close friend Ross; he knew my family situation and I knew he could help me deal with this mess.

Ross is a very insightful therapist who over the years helped me out of more jams than I can remember. Ross is someone that I like being around since he has a calm and reassuring demeanor. We are like siblings who tease each other yet we also are very supportive of one another.

"Ross, I am sorry about waking you up but I need your help. This is an emergency," I said.

"What's going on?" he asked alarmed.

I began to tell him what transpired last night.

"Karen, it is time to confront your brother. You need to be confident and strong! You need to let him know that you are on to him and he cannot get away with his behavior," he advised.

"I am scared, Ross," I said.

And then he gave me his advice and support, "You can do it. Leave the health club and go somewhere where no one can hear your conversation with him," he added.

So I left the club and drove to an isolated parking lot near my home. Before I called my brother I started to grunt louder and louder, as Ross suggested, bringing tension and energy into my body just as a sports player might do to prep for a game. This exercise felt extremely unnatural to me.

Then I called Barry and screamed at the top of my lungs (something which I rarely ever do), "You hurt me, I know what you tried to do. I know all about the damn penalties! I changed ownership of the CDs from your name into my name. If Daddy should pass away, you were not going to walk away with all the money!"

Barry was taken off guard and said, "What the hell are you talking about?"

"You know very well what I am talking about. I have asked you over the years if you ever took Daddy to get the will updated and you said no! You lied to me. In fact, you took him to the estate attorney that I recommended. I saw the updated will of 2005!" I screamed.

Shocked at my rage, Barry angrily said "I have another will to show you. I will come by in a few hours. I will drop it off and leave."

I said, "I will be waiting."

The phone went dead.

Another will? Now what? Damn, did I possibly miss another will in my father's files? Filled with apprehension, I had no choice but to wait. The next two hours drifted by so slowly. There was a knock on my front door and Barry walked in and slammed an envelope on my kitchen table. "Read this and you will have all your answers," he said, towering over me.

I opened it. Cautiously, I reviewed the contents. Barry still remained executor of the will but I was now going to receive fifty percent of the bequest. All the conditions of my inheritance were abated. Then I looked at the last page and noticed that it was updated this past November 2008. Coincidentally, that was one month after I fabricated the nightmare. Now it all makes sense, I thought, when I asked my father this past year about adding my name to his CDs, he agreed, because Barry had taken him to the estate attorney to redo the will at Thanksgiving.

Still angry, I said to Barry, "Why didn't you tell me about any of these wills? Why was I left in the dark? I had every right to know what was going on."

I didn't wait for a reply and continued, "Which will were you going to show me if Daddy should die? The old one or this updated version?"

My brother replied, "All these years Daddy kept telling me that you were stealing money from his accounts. He wanted me to come in all the time and take care of his finances. Now I understand his intentions. He was manipulating us against each other. He tried to sabotage our relationship so that he could be in control."

Twenty years after Jacob stole his brother's birthright and blessing he returned home to meet Esau. Jacob was predictably anxious and cautious and sent messengers ahead to tell Esau that was bringing gifts for him and his family. But the messengers returned saying Esau was planning to meet Jacob with four hundred men. Fearing an attack, Jacob divided his people into separate camps so that one might escape an assault. He prayed for assistance and sent numerous gifts to appease his brother.

The night prior to meeting Esau, Jacob was alone and wrestled with a man till daybreak. The man saw that he could not overpower Jacob and touched the socket of Jacob's hip, wrenching it as they continued to wrestle.

Then the man said, "Let me go, for it is daybreak."

But Jacob replied, "I will not let you go unless you bless me."

The man asked him, "What is your name?"

"Jacob," he answered.

Then the man said, "Your name will no longer be Jacob, but Israel, because you have struggled with God and with men and have overcome." Genesis 32:24-28

Jacob may have grappled with God or his conscience and finally awakened to a realization that he needed to "do the right thing." He had to learn one of the greatest lessons of his life before meeting Esau. Jacob had to first forgive himself for deceiving, lying and cheating his brother, and then he needed to ask forgiveness from Esau. At that moment, he decided to take ownership of his actions and awakened to a moment of clarity and authenticity. He stopped running away from his paralyzing fears and overcame them. He prevailed in his struggle and finally was at peace with himself.

Do I have the courage to forgive my brother? Or will I hang on to the past and let the pain eat away at me for years to come? Can I do the right thing?

Jacob and Esau greeted each other with tearful hugs and kisses rather than with swords. They both forgave each other and departed in peace. So in the end both Jacob and Esau made the right choice. The outcome of this scenario could have been devastating for the brothers, their families and the future generation of the children of Israel. I believe it was a testament to my opinion that any person can change for the better.

Barry was sitting at my kitchen table with the corrected will when he shared years of listening to our father accuse me of stealing. Me? At that moment I decided to forgive Barry and let go of all the anger I was harboring inside of me.

The stress from that entire year took a huge toll on my body; I wanted it to end with my brother and I reconciled. We understood that our father was to blame for all of the tension. I also realized that day that my father, too, had a change of heart (or Barry forced him, but I chose to go with the change-of-heart scenario). For whatever reason, he chose to update the will and make it equitable.

Today I can scrutinize my father's behavior and understand his motivations from a clearer perspective. His struggle to survive directed his life in its entirety. It ravaged his body and tormented his soul like a destructive hurricane destroying everything in its path. He existed in this survivor mode and behaved irrationally; he wanted to control everyone and everything in his life so he lied, cheated, stole, intimidated and created an unstable environment. He came from a world that demonstrated those very ideals in which people with power threatened, preyed upon and demanded submission from the young, frail and weak. He was quite efficient and relentless and as a result, my family suffered. How ironic that my father's behavior so closely mimicked the distorted ways of those who perpetrated the Holocaust. How heartbreaking that he was imprisoned all those years by his struggle to survive.

In 2011, a year after my father died, while cleaning my files, I came across the email I had sent Alisha about the hawk and the pigeon. I had completely forgotten about it. The hawk had been forced to fly out of its natural terrain to search for food; it killed only to survive. I felt like I'd also been forced out of my comfort zone and needed to stand up for myself by confronting my brother, for the security and survival of my family. As the hawk descended upon the pigeon, it looked barbaric, but it was a natural process. Anger is a natural and healthy emotion to display, but not for me. It was an extraordinarily difficult challenge to confront anyone. As a child I just wanted to escape from all the hostility and yelling in the house, so I hid in my bedroom closet to shut it all out. As an adult, I suppressed my anger and avoided circumstances that were confrontational; I would have rather walked away and estranged myself from both of them. Just as I thought the hawk was aggressive and horrible, I wouldn't be surprised if you, the reader, thought the same about what I did.

And my challenge didn't end with the confrontation; I had to figure out a way to forgive my brother, my father, and myself.

NINE

Waking Up

As he thinks in his heart, so he is.
-Jewish proverb

When I was nine years old, I vividly remember Howard bracing my father in a head lock position in the living room of our apartment. Howard was tall, broad, huge and overwhelmingly strong at fifteen years old, towering over my father. He yelled, "If you ever hurt Mommy again, I will kill you!"

That was the end of the physical abuse my mom had endured for quite some time.

It was March 2010, Bobby and I had been dating for over a year by then. I was at a neighborhood restaurant party when the hired photographer asked if he could take my picture and show it to one of his single friends, Bob, who is a widower. He thought we would make a great looking couple. He took my picture and within the week Bobby called me. On our second date, Bobby willingly disclosed that he is a child of Holocaust survivors. He knew very little about the details of his parents' experiences during the war, but shared everything he knew. It seemed that his identity as a Jew stemmed from his connection to the Holocaust, something that I have noticed in many of my friends who are children of survivors. I have never dated a child of a survivor and I wondered if this commonality we share is merely a coincidence. Bobby is very courteous, amiable and fun loving. Being very generous, he will be the first one to give you the shirt off his back; he has loaned money to several friends helping them out of financial difficulties. At six foot four, he often defended his friends when he was not able to divert a fight. He also happens to be a news, politics and sports junkie.

Bobby is always looking to go out and have fun. At a moment's notice, he'll pick me up on his motorcycle and we'll ride into downtown Chicago for a bite to eat. Yet, underneath this exterior is an underlying sadness and despair to his being, and a definite hardness when it comes to anyone who seems to defame or threaten the Jewish people or the State of Israel. He does not trust the Palestinians, Poles and countless other people of this world. He maintains a strong allegiance toward Israel and will vote for a U.S. candidate that seems to have the best relationship with Israel.

Just five months before my father passed away, Bobby and I went to see the new movie *Alice in Wonderland*. Alice was plummeting through the rabbit hole, a very lengthy, narrow, dark and terrifying space and ricocheting off the dirt walls. Barraged by a multitude of objects, she finally reached Underland, a very dreadful and frightful place.

That evening I had a very unusual dream. I was standing all alone in the middle of a vacant and monstrous-sized room with incredibly high ceilings. Suddenly, I was bombarded from above by massive household objects such as washing machines, beds, vacuum cleaners and sofas. It seemed that I was intentionally targeted and I was terrified of being harmed. I looked upward at the ceiling, but could not see anyone there. Maneuvering quickly, I dodged the massive objects as they fell all around me and I avoided being crushed to death. I felt a sense of relief and triumph that I survived this frightening ordeal. When I woke up, I recalled every sordid detail and feeling.

There was something markedly bothersome about this dream. Strangely, I had this succinct feeling that my father was responsible for all of these vicious attacks. That seemed odd. Why would I dream of my father intentionally trying to harm me? It was nonsensical.

Troubled by this peculiar dream, a week later I went to see my spiritual director, Colleen. I have been seeing her monthly for several years and during my visits, I talk about the events of my life, while she listens and accompanies me on my quest for truth and spiritual development. Colleen guided me through a meditation and I was redirected back to that dream; only this time I became the observer. In my meditation, I flew above the ceiling to watch myself and to understand how and why I was targeted. My father was sitting above the ceiling laughing as he maneuvered and rotated the levers of a machine that dropped the objects below. Finally, I came to the obvious conclusion that he simply was not cognizant I was below. I assumed that he just couldn't see me, so he didn't intentionally try to kill me. I felt relieved and satisfied with my analysis at that time.

A few months after my father died, I sat with Barry and asked him if he would like to share any memories of our father for this book. Barry gladly began to recall a story from his past. When he was fourteen, he was begging our father for money to purchase school books and as usual, our father refused. Barry noticed that Howard's wallet was out and filled with plenty of cash. Barry figured he would quietly borrow a twenty dollar bill from Howard and as soon as my father reimbursed him, he would slip the money back into Howard's wallet undetected. Well, Howard noticed the missing money and confronted Barry in front of our father. Barry confessed and explained his reasons, but Howard became enraged and began punching him. Barry vividly remembers that moment when he was lying on the floor being smacked by Howard; he looked up and saw our father laughing.

This story reminded me of my dream from six months before. I realized right then that my father had actually seen me, in my dream, and was taunting me from above. I finally understood that my father's behavior was deranged, mean spirited and downright evil. I was startled to hear myself describe my father in this manner, and I was hesitant to write it even though it is the stark truth. The fact that my father mistreated and inflicted pain on his own children is abominable, but when he derived pleasure and enjoyment from the brutality, well, I think that is perverse and wicked.

While writing this book, I started to uncover more symbolism in that pivotal dream. These household objects represent the madness and insanity that I confronted as a child in my home, all emanating from my father. The chaos was plentiful, unceasing, and I learned to avoid or maneuver my way around my father's barrage of craziness.

The way I coped with all of it was to avoid him whenever possible and to make myself invisible. He generally stayed away from me since there was always another family member to taunt in the house and engage in confrontation.

Interestingly, in my dream, one of the household objects that fell from the ceiling was a vacuum cleaner. My father had a nasty habit of grabbing the handle of the vacuum cleaner and whacking it at my mother when he was bored or crabby.

From Deceit to Awareness

Why didn't I remember all this? I was busy surviving, hiding, and too young to accept that my father behaved so viciously. I had the dream shortly before my father died; I truly didn't understand or accept the depth of his true character until he was dead.

This dream is accurate; he really did hide, he was secretive and deceitful. My father was shady and never forthright about his where-abouts. Concealing himself in the forests of Poland was invaluable to his survival. Exposing himself would make him vulnerable to being caught and killed. So he learned to hide and be sly. He continued to survive in this stealthy manner because this ultimately gave him the power to control everyone around him.

He was compelled to be this way; in fact, he was always paranoid about certain personal items and took a great deal of caution to always lock his desk drawer. He never allowed any of us in his bedroom and that included my mother. While growing up, my mother shared a bedroom with me. Below are a few excerpts from the love letters I found stashed away in the closet of his bedroom. This letter is from one of my father's mistresses written in 1999 after my father began communicating with her once again.

Dear Arie,
I am not involved with anyone else, nor have I been for the past 8 plus years. I go to dances, parties, socials, meetings, etc. but "goornish" (nothing). In fact, goornish minus -0-. I am looking for someone to share "my privacy" with. So if you come and visit, you will be king of the roost (just don't forget who is the queen). Of course I am not insulted not hearing from you all these years. I can only assume you are involved with someone else and don't have the decency and guts to tell me. I would like to see you again before you get involved with someone else. Once that happens we are out of each other's lives for good. You stuck by your marriage to the end, good, bad, or indifferent. I gave up on you when I left Chicago back in the early 1970s. I never dreamed you would write me when your wife was gone. I knew you would never leave Harriet no matter how unhappy you were. And let's not forget, I did meet you at a dance on a Saturday night at the Embassy Club in 1971 when your kids were very little. That has always been our secret and you can thank me for that. No matter how much of an ostrich you were, you were a cheater, just like Bill Clinton. You are lucky I was no Monica Lewinsky. Like I always told you, I had nothing to lose. I had no husband at the time, no children, no home, no business, no social standing; I was young, thin and pretty and always could support myself and then some. So let's not be critical if I should become lucky and become involved with someone before you get out here. It would sure be nice to have a local romance. Out here you can find yourself a wealthy widow, and I am sure you can in Chicago. Be it a "greena" (European) or an American. I recall you don't like the "green-a-tookis' (European woman's rear-end), but it might be hard to find an American gal who thinks the way you do. (Kosher, religious and frugal, and that's your good points)."
(Apparently my father had much to conceal.)
"Once again, Arie, I am requesting a copy of that big picture you and I took together at that Cafe-Europe at night. My ex-husband cut you off from that and I only have your arms around me while we posed at the bar. I pulled some other pictures of you and I in Las Vegas and Phoenix

back in the early 1970s. But I don't have my copy of that big picture and I believe it is the best one. Neither of us need it at this point, it's just something I would enjoy seeing again and it shouldn't cost you any money. I'm even enclosing a return envelope so it won't cost you the $.33 to mail. If you make a copy, I'll send you the cost, honest. I won't lose sleep over the cost of a photo reproduction as you might."

(It dawned on me that our family all traveled by car on a vacation from Chicago to Arizona and Nevada during that same time period. I never understood why my father would want to take us anywhere, let alone out west. My father was not interested in sightseeing or even searching for gold; apparently, he took us on a road trip to visit his girlfriend. Being too frugal to purchase a plane ticket, he was going to need assistance from Howard to drive across the country. When we reached our destination, he left my mother and us alone most of the time. It all makes sense now.)

"I found the pictures we took in Chicago dated Fall 1973 and in Phoenix and Scottsdale, Arizona in January 1975. Obviously that is the last time we saw each other. Are you still as good looking? I cannot answer for myself, you will have to judge, suffice it to say I now have silver black hair. The Suzie Bren is still there, but it's somewhat subdued in public. I am enclosing a photo taken three years ago at a wedding in Los Angeles.

I lost a lot of weight since then, but I was never as heavy as Harriet was when I saw her when I arrived to Chicago.

"Remember my trip to Greece, Turkey, Morocco, Spain, etc...., back in 1972. While I was gone you were cheating on me. It all seems so funny now. Does a leopard ever change his spots? I won't go for those schticks now, we're past that."

(The leopard's survivability in the wild is partially due to its stealthy hunting behaviors and its ability to adapt to its surroundings. It runs at great speeds and climbs high trees carrying its prey. Just as the leopard will kill any animal it can hunt down, my father will virtually hurt and harm anyone in his path that he considers a threat. My father, too, learned quickly to adapt to his surroundings as his clandestine behavior helped him survive. He was already living with Beba when he corresponded with this woman from twenty-five years before.

Why did he bother to keep all these letters, pictures and contact lists of these women? It was incriminating evidence.

It reminded me how detailed and methodical the Germans were at documenting all their war crimes, which eventually incriminated them. My father must have known that one day his children would eventually discover the letters. Maybe he wanted us to find them or maybe he just forgot.

Thanks to Arie Kaplan, I developed the ability to sense when someone is lying, manipulating, controlling and has abusive tendencies. Only recently have I understood why I have a strong aversion to people who exhibit these characteristics.)

Survival and Triumph

My survival: in addition to everything I learned from the dream, I recognized a familiar theme. The history of my people is a continuing story of survival and triumph. I, too, survived the evil tyrant, who plotted to physically destroy me in my dream.

In my home as a young child, I never experienced any physical abuse since my mother made it perfectly clear to my father that he is not to lay one finger on me. But I witnessed my father physically abusing my mother and brothers. Verbal abuse toward everyone in my home was always plentiful.

I managed to survive the barrage of unpredictable madness by shielding myself in my bedroom, my place of refuge. All I wanted was to be left alone. However, all too frequently, some family member would barge into my room uninvited, exploding and spewing their insanity into my sacred space like a volcano purging its insides onto its surroundings. As I tried to avoid the tumult and detach from all the toxic and useless arguments, I was fearful and on high alert waiting for the unforeseen moment when my father would explode and the chaos would soon erupt again.

My fears extended to the outside world as I was always vigilant of my surroundings never knowing when someone skulking in the shadows may attack. As a child, I recall sitting in the synagogue (especially during the High Holidays when the sanctuary was filled to capacity), or during my school assemblies or Jewish community gatherings, thinking these would be ideal situations for our anti-Semitic enemies to strike. Sitting near exit doors to quickly escape would be useless since we would have all been barricaded inside. I thought this was a perfectly normal way of thinking.

Just recently, I finally understood that my "startle reflex" is a direct connection of my past. My body indiscriminately reacts, whether it is at home sitting quietly in a room or out in a crowded public place. I react when an unexpected stimulus such as a loud noise, or a quick jerky movement, comes into my space or near my face. Depending on the level of panic, my body immediately ripples a spasm of shock. As my arm and leg muscles contract, my heart races and my breathing intensifies; I begin to quiver with tremors and then emit a loud shriek, usually scaring anyone in my vicinity. Anything that may sneak up on me like a cat, dog, insect or my son just standing in the hallway of my home will create this reaction.

Late one night, Bobby and I were at the supermarket; he went to buy the coffee and I went to the ethnic aisle. I stood there focusing on reading the ingredients of a jar of spaghetti sauce. Bobby came up from behind and lovingly whispered hello into my ear. I shrieked and threw the jar into the air. Chunky red sauce and broken glass splattered over the floor and Bobby quickly learned never to sneak up on me again. It is interesting to note that soldiers and victims of war have post-traumatic stress disorder (PTSD) and will often exhibit this startle response. I never knew I had been traumatized until my body in its wisdom showed me that I carry the traits of a survivor of the Holocaust.

As an adult I have always introduced myself as a "child of a Holocaust survivor". There was something that compelled me to publicly expose and acknowledge this part of myself, just as Jews were forced to wear round yellow patches and yellow hats in medieval Europe or sew the yellow Star of David on their outer garments during the Holocaust. My identity as a child of a survivor was so much a part of me that it felt almost like an extra limb on my body.

I know I survived the chaos, my father's negligence, his abuse, and everything else, but I continued to be afflicted by it all. The way I clung to irrational thoughts, the unforgiving way I treated myself and others, and my ongoing loneliness proved ultimately that I hadn't overcome the fear and anguish of little me. I thought everything was normal; it was only much later that I wondered how I'd lived without calmness, compassion or love. I survived my childhood, but did I triumph?

My father's survival: my father understood that he was born into a legacy of age-old anti-Semitism and came from a long line of scapegoats. He spoke disdainfully about the domination of the Germans and Poles, the aggressors of society, and how they demanded submission from the feeble and powerless Jews. They preyed over his people like a vulture that seldom attacks the strong and healthy animals but focuses on killing the wounded, weak and sickly ones. During the war it was quite clear to my father that he had to kill or be killed! In his view, being cunning and self-absorbed meant life and being kind and altruistic meant death. However, when the war ended he continued to think, feel and behave according to this rationale; exactly the opposite of what is valued in normal, healthy society.

I think that natural assertiveness and strength are protective and admirable characteristics to embody when they are connected to love. But my father embodied the shadowed side of these traits since he was completely out of touch with himself, and disconnected from truly loving anyone. He became the aggressor he disdained, the least respected in the synagogue in which he dreamed of respect, and although he longed for control, he was only able to force it upon his wife and children. He lived a long life full of fear that he both felt and created for others.

For 65 years after the war, until he died, he was trapped in a distorted inner world. He, too, survived, but did he triumph?

My people's survival: when the Dalai Lama met Elie Wiesel several years ago he said, "Your people suffered a lot and you went into exile 2,000 years ago, but you are still here. My people just left our homeland; we are in exile. Teach us how to survive."

Wiesel responded, "When we left Jerusalem, we didn't take all our jewels with us. All we took was a little book. It was the book that kept us alive. Second, because of our exile we developed a sense of solidarity. When Jews left one place for the next, there were always Jews to welcome and take care of them. And, third, good memory. Survival takes a good memory."

Dr. Rachel Yehuda, Professor of Psychiatry and Neurobiology at the Mount Sinai School of Medicine, was working in a clinic treating and studying aging Holocaust survivors. Surprisingly, the children of these survivors requested to be studied and treated, as well. Yehuda discovered that the children of Holocaust survivors exhibited statistically higher than expected rates of Post-Traumatic Stress Disorder (PTSD) and she assumed it to be from the barrage of horrific stories they heard growing up. But her research demonstrated that low levels of the hormone cortisol were found in both the survivors and their children's urine. The function of cortisol is to enable the body to physically handle stressful and threatening situations like fight or flight; reduced cortisol levels lower the ability of the body to handle these situations. Yehuda concluded that the retelling of the stories was not the reason why the children had PTSD, rather it was due to their low cortisol levels. Yehuda explained that the trauma of the Holocaust created epigenetic changes within the survivors that were passed along to their offspring. The children then exhibited similar characteristics to their parents.[2]

Interestingly, my daughter has startle reflex, too. When we are at home and she quietly and casually walks into my room, she unknowingly scares me and I belt out a scream. Then she gets scared and shrieks. Once we both calm down, we laugh it off. My sons do not experience any of these symptoms but when Noah was younger he would quietly stand in the hallway waiting for me to pass by and was amused when I screamed.

There is a field of study called epigenetics that looks at the heritable changes in gene expression caused by various environmental factors. These changes are subsequently passed down to a person's offspring

---

2   Bower, Bruce. "Trauma Syndrome Traverses Generations." *Science News* 149(1996). Online.

Yehuda, Rachel, Ph.D.; Bierer, Linda M., M.D.; Schmeidler, James, Ph.D.; Aferiat, Daniel H., M.S.W.; Breslau, Ilana, M.A.; Dolan, Susan, B.A. "Low Cortisol and Risk for PTSD in Adult Offspring of Holocaust Survivors." *The American Journal of Psychiatry*, Volume 157, No. 8, August 2000:1229-1235. Print.

Yehuda, Rachel, Ph.D.; Schmeidler, James, Ph.D.; Wainberg, Milton, M.D.; Binder-Brynes, Karen, Ph.D.; Duvdevani, Tamar, B.A. "Vulnerability to Posttraumatic Stress Disorder in Adult Offspring of Holocaust Survivors." *The American Journal of Psychiatry* 1998:1163-1171. Print.

keeping the sequence of the DNA intact. The DNA is governed by the epigenome or a switch that allows the DNA to turn on or off the genetic expression. Environmental factors that can greatly influence the epigenome are trauma, diet and exercise. The trauma of living through the Holocaust can certainly trigger the epigenome thus changing the genetic expression for the offspring. In turn this genetic expression continues to be passed down from generation to generation. In other words, the mental and physical diseases that we carry today may be a direct result of our parents', grandparents' and great grandparents' traumatic lives. [3]

The study of genetics encourages us to think that evolutionary changes occur over millions of years, while the study of epigenetics provides us with an understanding that changes can occur in the very next generation.

The summarized responses from Yehudah's interviews with the children of the survivors peaked my interest because they too were all deeply affected by their parent(s) Holocaust experiences.

The children of these survivors said that they felt different and damaged. I always felt that my brothers were damaged because their personalities were just a bit off, and I was the "normal" child in my family. I thought they were more affected by my father than I was; after all he beat them at least weekly and never touched me.

I think that after generations of suffering, those who are connected to Judaism carry the burden of suffering in our DNA just like the children of Holocaust survivors have lower concentrations of cortisol in their blood. We're also overwhelmingly concerned with the survival of our people. It is as if we inherited traits, emotions, and behaviors accumulated over three millennium along with genetic mutations like Tay Sachs or Gaucher's Disease.

As a people, we are understandingly damaged by our afflicted past. We are not only children of Holocaust survivors but we come from a long line of ancestors who survived centuries of persecution, terror, war and destruction.

---

3 Cloud, John. 'Why Your DNA isn't Your Destiny." *Time* January 6, 2012. Online. Genetic Science Learning Center. "Epigenetics and Inheritance." Learn.Genetics 3 December 2012 <http://learn.genetics.utah.edu/content/epigenetics/inheritance/>

I think all this history of suffering became part of our collective being and continues to impact our collective identity, our Jewish values, and how we relate to the world. We cope with our trauma by exhaustively focusing our attention and energies on topics of persecution as if we are re-experiencing the trauma today here in 21st-century America. Anti-Semitism continues to exist in certain places of the world, including here in the United States, just as hatred of one people for another has always existed in all parts of the world.

Here are some examples of our post-traumatic stress disorder:
- We become easily startled or agitated by flashing new events.
- Stress, angst and paranoia surface, especially when we are exposed to current community and worldwide events that are connected to or symbolize our past trauma.
- We are constantly on heightened alert to our surrounding communities of the world and we compulsively dwell on anti-Semitism. So we rally downtown and unite when we perceive peril to our people around the world.
- Any comment an individual or political official makes about the Jews or Israel is overly scrutinized and will generally be perceived as anti-Semitic.

Yet today my rabbi wrote in a letter to our congregation after meeting Joe Biden, the Vice President of the United States, saying, "During World War Two it was almost impossible for leaders of the Jewish Community to meet with President Roosevelt, but now at AIPAC (The American Israel Public Affairs Committee) and even the Rabbinical Assembly, our leaders come to us." We have been elected into prominent positions in this country: mayors of major cities, (Chicago and New York) congressman, senators, Secretary of State, head of the Federal Reserve and part of the Presidential Cabinet.

We continue to believe that we are the victims of the world and we must watch our backs. The private Jewish elementary day school where my children were educated has no sign on their property bearing its name. The school does not want to attract attention.

A lecture this past May 2012, at a Chicago city college on "anti-Semitism on campus" was not advertised in any of the campus papers. Heavy security was in place but there were no outsiders who came to protest.

When spiritual leaders speak their hateful rhetoric, as they have done for years, we are alarmed. When they show their support, we are skeptical. When I attended an APAIC meeting, an African American minister spoke and on behalf of his community and colleagues, he pledged his support to the Jewish community and Israel. Bobby said, "I don't believe him." Some of my friends tell me that they have guns in their homes for fear of another Holocaust.

There is a fine line between acting cautiously and acting in fear. We may choose to negate these thoughts and feelings and consider them to be innocuous, just as I have done so personally with my own life, but they are there hovering over us like a shadow of darkness.

Many of us may not concur with this perspective because we might feel we are a financially successful people consisting of distinguished professionals and highly respected citizens of our homelands. But, we carry with us these burdens of our past and pass them along to the next generation.

Some children of survivors in the Yehuda study explained that they had been too young to digest the extensive violent details of the war when their parents exposed their painful past to them.

My girlfriend Lisa told me that as early as kindergarten, her mother, a Holocaust survivor and widow, would burden her with horrifying stories of her life during the war. Lisa felt that she missed out on being kid and instead became a consoler to her mother. As an adult, Lisa finally confronted her mother and told her to see a therapist. Her mother said that if she cannot speak to her own daughter, she was unwilling to share her past with anyone else. In my view, Lisa continues to put herself in the position of listening to people's problems, without being able to extricate herself from uncomfortable situations.

Our community has diligently exposed every horrific detail of our horrendous past to the next generation. We molded our fears onto our young, encumbering their psyche with the psychoses of our past. Can we ever learn to let go of our fears? If so, will our identity as a people change? Who might we become? Is it possible to educate our children from a spiritual and loving angle?

In Yehuda's study, some of these children of survivors reported that they experienced emotional and physical neglect growing up and also endured physical and sexual abuse. One day while talking to my cousin Jerry, he said, "Hitting children was a common and acceptable mode of punishment by our parents' generation in Europe. They were tougher on kids in the old country. By age thirteen, a young boy in Europe would often be forced out of his home to search for work in efforts to bring money and food into the household. Food was scarce and the young men needed to pull their own weight. I remember when my mother smacked me several times in front of my teacher here in the Chicago public schools. Once she struck me so hard I landed on the floor with the wind knocked out of me."

Barry recalled a story from our upbringing and asked me, "Karen, do you remember when we took classes at the Jewish Community Center (JCC) after school?"

I nodded and said, "We would wait for Daddy to pick us up at 5:00 p.m. sharp. I remember always being dressed and ready for him."

Barry said, "One day the art teacher at the JCC suggested I try a new class and I forgot to keep track of the time. At 5:30 p.m., Daddy marched into the art room and threw me on the floor. Then he yelled, kicked and punched me in front of the teacher and my friends."

Barry was very upset as he told this story and continued on with one more. "I am not sure if you were ever aware of what was really going on in the house between our parents. You were too little to understand."

"What are you talking about?" I asked.

"You know that Daddy always kept his master bedroom to himself. Well, one night Howard and I overheard him speak to Mommy in a demanding tone. He said 'Come to my room tonight.' Well, we both understood his intent. He wanted sex with her and she had no choice but to follow his orders. She was afraid of him."

"I never realized this was happening," I said.

Barry continued on and said that one evening he overheard our father repeat those words again. Barry raised his voice and said that he knew what was going on. Our mother was terribly embarrassed and said to our father not to mention this in front of the kids anymore. He became angry and told her he didn't give a damn and told her to go to hell. After that incident, when he wanted sex on any given night, he left his bedroom door open."

I felt like throwing up. I wondered what she thought and how she felt every time she went unwillingly into his bedroom at night. How many nights did she spend all alone crying herself to sleep? Was she just a body to him where he could relieve himself? I cried myself to sleep that night.

I believe the only way my mother managed to escape from his abuse was to become physically unappealing to him so she continued to gain an inordinate amount of weight. Though food became her salvation, it also was deleterious to her health. Her excessive weight (300 pounds) inhibited her from doing many day-to-day activities and possibly caused or exacerbated her uterine cancer.

I began to think about the symbolism of her rare form of cancer. The function of the uterus is to provide a nurturing environment to protect and shelter the developing fetus thereby bringing a healthy baby into the world. My mother never felt safe, nurtured or loved in her own home; my cousin thought she lived in a state of hysteria. I believe that the stress took a toll on her body. She had a complete hysterectomy, but it was too late to save her life; the cancer had viciously metastasized.

Thirteen years later just prior to my father's death, I, too, was stressed out by feelings of betrayal and worrying about the financial future of my family. Four massive fibroids were growing inside of me and I was suffering a huge amount of discomfort. Just a couple of months before my father passed away, I was forced into surgery to have my uterus removed.

While writing this book, I shared my painful childhood stories with friends who are children of survivors. Many freely opened up and shared the verbal, emotional and sexual abuse experiences of their homes. As late as a few decades ago, our Jewish community as a whole thought it was immune from abuse and alcoholism. Shalva opened its doors in 1986, serving thousands of Jewish battered women and children each year within the Chicago area.

In Yehuda's study many of the children of Holocaust survivors felt that their lives were belittled by their parent(s) because they hadn't suffered as their parents had. These children said that they were accused of not acknowledging the sacrifices their parents had made for them. Just to prove his valor and respect, my cousin Jerry volunteered to serve in Vietnam. He came home a broken man, but his mother still did not think he understood what it means to suffer.

Some of these children of survivors felt that their parents tried to create a normal and nurturing environment in their homes by letting go of the past. However, the fears of an anti-Semitic world consumed these survivors. They felt that everything could be taken from them instantaneously so they lived like my family. They always had some hidden cash, updated passports and hoarded food, "just in case."

Last summer in 2011, one year after my father died, I went to close up an old account from one of my father's banks in West Rogers Park. I chatted with Ron, the bank manager who always made a sincere effort to get to know all his customers. Ron was Jewish and married to a non-Jewish woman. We sat in his office and he shared this story: "A rabbi sat down in my office when he heard that my father had recently died of cancer. He offered his sincere condolences; but, I will never forgive him for what he said."

"What could he possibly have said to make you so upset?" I asked.

"Well, first he asked me if I was saying Kaddish for my dad and I replied, no. He then said that the cost for hiring someone to pray daily for my father was $1,200.00 but he offered me a deal for $700.00."

I said, "That is the custom. He believes that if a family member is not able to say the prayers for the departing soul, then someone should be hired to recite the prayers."

"It was what he said next that really upset me. Under his breath he said, 'cancer should only happen to the goyim (non-Jews).'"

This man is full of anger and resentment, I thought. He reminded me of the way my father spoke about the non-Jews. This community is still caught up in the struggle of survival.

It was just a few years ago that I finally understood my aversion to lengthy car rides, especially in the southern regions of the United States. I never forget certain images I saw on TV during my childhood of the Ku Klux Klansman parading around at night in their white robes, white conical hats and masks carrying the burning wood crosses terrorizing Blacks and Jews. They lived incognito as sheriffs, judges, gas station attendants, storekeepers, etc. occupying key positions in small towns. God forbid, my car breaks down in one of these remote places; I may not come out alive.

Some of my closest girlfriends spoke about how their fears impacted their personal relationships, making intimacy quite difficult. In religious school, I learned that marriage was about insuring the lineage of my people, and propagating the next generation of Jews. "Peru Orvu" (be fruitful and multiply) is the first commandment of the Torah and it is the one that insures our survivability. Though I certainly hoped that love and intimacy would somehow find its way into my marriage, it never did. I was 23; I didn't understand intimacy and didn't have any role models in my life, except for my parents and teachers who all spoke incessantly about the importance of Jewish continuity.

Earlier one day in October, 2009, my father walked from Beba's apartment to his psychiatrist's office in Uptown for his regular checkup. The doctor's staff wanted to make sure that my father had a ride home and would not let him leave the office. My father was having difficulty understanding them because of his hearing loss and became agitated. Instead of trying to communicate to him in writing, slowing their speech or calling me, the receptionist reported a serious problem and the psychiatrist sent him to the hospital psychiatric ward against his will. Bobby's first and only time he met my father was when he accompanied me to the unit that evening so I could attempt to release my father. We waited for him in a tiny corner room on the hospital floor. I sat at the small table and Bobby sat behind me against the wall. Soon my father appeared, dressed in a hospital gown covered by his worn out sweater along with hospital slippers. The staff had taken his dentures and the rest of his clothes. He was terrified and very upset. He sat down at the table and glared at Bobby. Instead of demanding to be freed immediately from the psych ward, I knew my father was going to focus on Bobby. He asked me in Yiddish, "Who is that man sitting behind you?"

I replied loudly, "He is my boyfriend."

"Is he Jewish?" my father asked.

"Yes", I answered, "he is a child of survivors."

"Good, now get me out of this meshugoyim haus (insane asylum)," he yelled.

He was there for a week until I was able to have him released.

He was nearly traumatized from this experience; he called me each day terribly upset that they refused to return his teeth and his other belongings. My father was consumed with the fear of extermination and living as if he was about to be taken. This experience in the hospital was the exact nightmare he'd always dreaded and anticipated.

I believe the responses from these children of Holocaust survivors in New York City are representative of children of Holocaust living in the United States, Israel, Europe, South America, Australia and worldwide, as well as the children whose parents fled their homes and escaped persecution in Europe several years prior to World War II.

Surviving is quite different from living triumphantly. Triumph is when we no longer see ourselves as victims. As long as we identify ourselves as survivors, we keep on existing as if we're about to lose our freedom. We as a community have struggled far too long and deserve to live in peace, but we are teetering between a world of victimization and a world of liberation.

The Hebrew word "Shalom" means peace and is derived from the word "Shalem" meaning complete. When we are complete within ourselves nurturing healthy feelings of peace, love and joy, we can create a fulfilling existence. We will have a deeper understanding of ourselves, strengthen our relationship with others and create an authentic relationship with God, truly living up to our name: The people of Israel.

Oseh shalom bimromav, hu ya ase shalom alenu v'al kol yisra'el, v'imru Amen.

May the One who causes peace to reign in the high heavens let peace descend on us and on all Israel, and let us say: Amen.

We have survived as a people, but have we triumphed?

TEN

A Path of Truth

We do not attract what we want but who we are.
- James Lane Allen

In July 1997, while my mother remained hospitalized during the final six weeks of her life, Barry and I were constantly at her side, day and night.

On this particular day she was scheduled for a hysterectomy and exploratory surgery and we escorted her up to the doors of the surgical unit. As she lay on the stretcher bed, we held her hands, kissed her on her cheeks and attempted to reassure her that everything would be all right. Barry and I were nervous but we did our best to compose ourselves. My father happened to be with us that day. My mother clearly understood that this might have been her final waking moment and she trembled with fear. I will never forget when she glanced into my father's eyes; she hoped to hear my father say some words of endearment...a few gentle words of goodbye. My father stood there, silently nodded his head but didn't say a single word. I saw her devastation. I truly hated my father at that moment; he could have said, "I love you" or "you'll be fine" or a number of nice endearments.

My mother survived the surgery but died one week later. She was in and out of consciousness and passed away knowing that Barry and I loved her.

When I was young I overheard my mother once yell at my father that she hoped he had some love for himself because no one in this world loved him. The sad truth was that my father isolated himself from any love inside of him and, therefore, could not offer love to anyone else. Love did not protect his family when the Ukrainians and Poles came to murder them. Love did not keep him safe or warm when he was hunted by the Nazis and trying to survive three brutal winters in the forests. And love certainly did not save his first-born son from dying an unexpected early death. So love was useless and expressing any kind words was senseless to him.

Today I believe my father may have struggled in that moment as he faced my mother on her death bed. Triggered by his past, all he could do was shut himself down. Perhaps he thought that life continued to prove itself ardently cruel to him.

A few days after September 11, 2001, I listened to the news broadcast of several phone conversations of victims on the airplane that plummeted from the sky and those trapped in the Twin Towers. With only minutes to spare, they called their loved ones and the words they said during their phone calls were those three precious words. Strangely, I envied those victims who perished that day. They were given the opportunity to say "I love you" in their final moments of their life. They were blessed with hearing their spouses utter those three heartfelt words in return without any hesitation. At that despairing moment in their lives, their love was undoubtedly confirmed and genuinely received. They modeled a love that was non-existent in my childhood home or my marriage. They shared a gift that I had longed for in my life. They were all so fortunate.

When I thought back then about whom I would call to say my final goodbyes, I realized it was not going to be my husband. This realization forced me to face the truth that I was not going to stay in a relationship that lacked love. I was not going to spend the rest of my life living with someone tossing a few bread crumbs of pseudo-love at me every once in a while. I was not going to lie on my death bed deceiving myself and thinking that my relationship with my husband was an authentic loving one. I certainly was not going to repeat my mother's life. My parents' relationship was everything I did not want in my life.

I am grateful to my parents and to those victims of 9/11, who unknowingly helped give me clarity, graced me with courage and directed me to a path of truth. May their memories be a blessing.

Conversing with my father was generally unpleasant. When we did engage in conversation, it was generally about adhering to the laws of Judaism, the rising of anti-Semitism and keeping vigil with money. Any other topic was inconsequential to him. There was never a "Good Morning, how are you feeling?" or "How was school today?" When I graduated high school and college, there was never a Mazel Tov. I remember the day when I was 22 years old, that I told my father I was engaged. He stared at me, nodded his head and left the room.

He would often say to my brothers and me, "Keep the Sabbath and keep kosher. Hitler tried to exterminate us and we cannot let him defeat us. Do not deviate from the traditions or we vill become extinct. Stay avay from the goyim (non-Jews)...the schvartzes (Negroes), Mexicans and Japanese are all no good. You must not marry them. We must survive as a people."

Then he would point his index finger at us and add, "If you break away from our traditions and marry outside the faith, I vill have nothing to do with you. You vill be cut out of my life."

Even though I knew my father was a hypocrite, and often transgressed the laws, I still hoped that he would love me for practicing them diligently. Maybe if I followed them perfectly, he would not find any fault in me. Maybe if I observed them better than he did, he would love me. As

I grew older, I became aware that nothing would ever satisfy him no matter how perfectly I tried. As an adult, I realized that the traditional belief system of rules I followed was not spiritually gratifying. My soul was crying for change. So I slowly shed my ingrained childhood observances, one by one, feeling liberated from being restricted to a way of life that was not serving me anymore. By the year 2000, I was no longer keeping kosher and attending weekly Shabbat services and my father became infuriated. He was upset and said that I was mocking his past, defying my religion and betraying my people.

Longing to gain a deeper sense of meaning in my life, I decided to apply to a Spiritual Direction internship; I wanted to become a spiritual director. Because there were no Jewish programs of this sort in the Chicago area, I attended the Claret Center in Hyde Park, Chicago, beginning in the fall of 2006. My class consisted of nine Catholics and one Presbyterian. I was the sole Jew. In this class were two Franciscan priests, one theologian, two students completing their Master's degrees at Chicago Theological Union (CTU), two nuns, one college counselor and two lay people all enhancing their profession or futures with Spiritual Direction. It was led by two elderly nuns who had spent their lives as educators and spiritual directors.

Prior to the start of the internship, our group of interns attended a weekend retreat during which we shared our varied backgrounds, life challenges and future aspirations. I vividly remember when Sister Maria from Rwanda told her story. In 1994, she studied in France completing her Master's degree in Educational Sciences when she learned of the Rwandan genocide. When she returned to her country, she discovered that her brother was the only survivor of her family; her parents and the rest of her siblings had been murdered. She came to study at the Claret Center for a year to improve her skills as a spiritual leader and learn to be more sensitive to the people of Rwanda who survived the genocide. When Maria finished speaking, only I stood up and embraced her, crying for what she'd endured. But I was puzzled at the absence of heaviness, anguish and anger that I would have shown in her position. Sister Maria had undergone so much pain and suffering, yet she seemed unburdened by her difficult memories. I was the one crying at her story while she stood dry-eyed comforting me in her arms. Where was her anger and pain? Where was her victim mentality? She seemed undefeated, held herself with dignity and moved gracefully. I was awed by her calm and untroubled demeanor, and inspired by her devotion to helping and healing her people.

As the months progressed, I became friends with many of the interns. Before we adjourned for winter break, we celebrated with a Hanukah and Christmas party, shared some holiday traditions, singing songs and enjoying a holiday meal.

One night during winter break, I happened upon the movie *The Sound of Music* on television. As I watched one of the final scenes in which the nuns aided the Von Trapp family from the Nazis by hiding them in the graveyard of the abbey, my fears of safety and survival in this country were stirred. If a Holocaust should occur in America, would my clergy friends from the Claret Center help my family? I thought that surely my new friends would protect my children and me, perhaps hiding us in their parishes and homes.

The internship continued and soon Passover and Easter were just one week away. At lunchtime many of us gathered and ate together at the center, as it gave us the opportunity to talk casually about current events, family issues and religion. On the last day of class before Spring break, one of the interns asked me to explain the Jewish dietary laws. After I discussed at great length the types of kosher animals, slaughtering rituals, kosher package symbols, rabbinical supervision and the laws of separating milk and meat, I mentioned that the price of kosher meat and chicken was exceedingly expensive. The Filipino theologian responded, "Jews can afford it, they are rich."

The Franciscan priest (working at the University of Illinois) added, "On the downstate campus, the Illini Tower dormitory is the most expensive place for room and board and is comprised of mostly Jewish students."

Appalled at these remarks, I looked around to see if anyone thought they were offensive. I locked eyes with Kerin, one of the lay Catholic students, who was noticeably uncomfortable but said nothing. No one said anything. So I carefully stated, "Not all Jews are rich. We are a community like everyone else. We have many poor families struggling to make ends meet and there are many senior citizens who desperately need aid.

As a matter of fact, Jews will be gathering to box and deliver thousands of food packages this week to aid the poor Jewish families throughout the Chicago metropolitan area who cannot afford to make a Passover meal."

Again, no one responded. Within minutes lunch had ended and everyone stood up to return to class as if nothing had happened. I turned to Eugenia, the other lay Catholic woman, and quietly said, "Can you believe the disparaging remarks that were made regarding Jews and money?"

She casually replied, "Oh that comment..... that was nothing."

Nothing? My body froze and I sat in shock, disbelieving what I'd heard, glued to my chair. The bell rang, and everyone rose but I hesitated to return to class and had trouble standing up. After a few minutes I forced myself out of the chair, and slowly walked into the classroom. I sat down, but I couldn't focus on whatever the teacher was saying. Instead, I keenly stared at each intern and wondered if any were truly my friends. Their remarks were offensive and not one of them had uttered a single word of apology or remorse.

After class I had a scheduled appointment with one of the directors, during which I reiterated the entire story. I told her that I felt truly betrayed and abandoned by people I thought were my friends. Not only that, these interns were spiritual seekers, leaders and healers of their churches and communities; I had expected respect from them. She listened, nodded, and said that she would call me after discussing the issue with her colleagues. She had tears of empathy in her eyes, so I agreed to hold off on making a decision to leave the program.

During the spring break, I grappled with whether or not to continue the program. The trust, security, and respect I'd felt for my fellow interns seemed to have vanished. I could not imagine spending the rest of the year with them. On the other hand, why should I quit the program and give up on my personal aspirations? My Claret advisor called to assure me that she'd support me if I wished to share my dismay at what happened. I decided to not let anything get in my way of completing the program, and returned to the Claret Center after spring break with some trepidation. I felt extremely fragile as I sobbed my way through the story and felt devastated once again. Many of the interns looked at me with surprise, astounded to hear me evoke such strong feelings. I finished speaking and nervously waited for their replies.

First, the Franciscan priest who commented about the University dormitory said, "I didn't mean anything by that comment. It was just an observation." It's possible that he didn't hate Jews, but I was relatively sure that both his immediate reaction to my comments and his lame apology indicated either prejudice or ignorance.

Then the middle-aged African American woman studying for her Master's degree softly spoke and said, "I'm sorry, Karen. I am all too familiar with your story. I understand what it feels like to be singled out and a victim of prejudice. I, regretfully, did not have the courage to speak on your behalf."

Another Master's degree candidate cried, saying, "I feel horrible that I was so insensitive. I'm sorry, Karen." I thought he probably never faced discrimination in his own life and was unable to understand my distress, but his was a heartfelt apology.

Then the Filipino theologian who made the first disparaging remark said, "I'm really sorry. I know how it feels to be a victim. When the recent story developed in the news about the Virginia Tech massacre, I prayed the shooter was not going to be Asian. I, too, am a victim of prejudice and could never perpetuate prejudice against anyone else." Then he sobbed, and even though I forgave him, I don't think that being a victim of bigotry automatically prevents a person from becoming a bigot. My father was a perfect example of how being the brunt of bigotry can promote bigotry.

The woman pursuing a career in lay ministry said, "I was the one who justified the original comments by saying that they meant nothing. I'm sorry, because the comments were offensive and my excusing them was also offensive. I hope you can forgive me." She told me afterwards that she was also sorry that she didn't confront the Filipino theologian after his first remark.

The other woman in lay ministry, who had linked eyes with mine, excused herself with, "Karen, I remember noticing that you were uncomfortable but thought that you stood up for yourself remarkably well. There was nothing more I could have added." The college counselor, to my surprise, didn't say anything. Neither of these women apologized or validated my feelings, so those relationships fizzled, but they clearly weren't my friends from the beginning.

Those who hadn't been at the devastating lunch discussion stayed silent, and I understood that Sister Maria didn't participate because she did not comprehend the quick pace of our lunchroom conversation.

Speaking out against hatred and prejudice is an extremely important value of mine. Even after the world understood that the Third Reich had a 'final solution' for the Jews, most of the world stayed silent. Forty years later, the world allowed the ethnic cleansing and displacement of millions of Bosnian citizens out of what had been Yugoslavia. People must speak against any kind of discrimination if we want to avoid the end results that we've seen far too many times. What happened to me was a tiny incident, but I think that accepting even small amounts of prejudice is both unacceptable and potentially harmful in a healthy society.

It would have been easier to withdraw from the internship and abstain from sharing my feelings with everyone. Avoiding personal confrontation and remaining stagnant in my emotional pain was my pattern in life. But I decided that I was not going to settle again for feeling closed off, resentful and heavy hearted. I spoke up, I accepted apologies, and I let go of the pain; I forgave them. From that day onward, many of the interns made continuous efforts to be more sensitive to me. I was glad not to have more hate and bitterness to store in my body; I already carried enough.

Today, as I reflect on my experience at Claret from a clearer and non-emotional perspective, I realize that my reaction to the interns was exacerbated by my own deep-seated fears and paranoia. My background led me to have a heightened sensitivity to all seemingly prejudicial comments so that when I thought I heard them, I reacted quickly in the most negative way. I believe most Jews connected to Judaism also share an inordinate amount of fear and paranoia. We are a people determined to ask questions and search for answers yet we have not sufficiently questioned, discussed and analyzed these paranoia and fears. As descendants of those who have suffered, we have unknowingly created a paradigm based on their, not our, suffering. Then we make the suffering our reality. Although it's not the truth we continue to assume and build upon generations of paranoia and fear. As these deeply embedded paranoia and fears have passed from generation to generation, our minds, bodies and spirits have been traumatized, making our lives less than they could be. Those spiritual leaders who continue to speak from a place of fear and paranoia by scolding and condemning their congregations are making sure that their congregants adhere to the rules without fostering their relationships to God and others in their community. When our community leaders focus on survival without growth, anti-Semitism without respect for others, and intra-faith negativity instead of dialogue, we have lost the essence of Judaism's Golden rule. "The stranger who resides with you shall be to you as one of your citizens; you shall love him as yourself, for you were strangers in the land of Egypt: I the Lord am your God." Leviticus 19:34

As an example, In May 2012, I attended the annual AIPAC event in Chicago, along with 1,300 others who care about Israel. I was struck by the words of the keynote speaker, Tal Becker, a senior advisor to then-foreign minister Tzipi Livni and a lead negotiator in Israeli-Palestinian negotiations during the Annapolis peace process, who noted something to the effect that "We are a traumatized people." I agreed with him when he said that when we use the words "existential threat" every six seconds, our enemies hear it, and think they have a chance.

Not all truths are valid for all generations all the time.

I think that we create our own destiny which begins with our beliefs as are taught in the teachings of Kabbalah, an ancient set of mystical beliefs of Judaism. A belief is the psychological state in which an individual holds a proposition or premise to be true. So what one believes may not be the truth, but if one believes it is the truth, then one will live accordingly and manifest a world around that belief system.

My Jewish community believes with all our hearts, with all our souls and with all our might that we will encounter anti-Semitism in every generation.

And we do.

We believe with all our hearts, with all our souls and with all our might that pain and suffering will be inflicted upon us.

And it is.

We believe with all our hearts, with all our souls and with all our might that we will survive. God will protect us and never abandon us no matter how difficult life becomes.

And we survive.

To all of you who are pounding on your tables recalling recent attacks on synagogues and Jews in France, Iranian rhetoric about their goal to destroy Israel and all the isolated incidents around the world, please be assured that I know hatred exists everywhere. Because we are Jews, we are more sensitive to acts of hatred against our own, and may not be conscious or spend little time anguishing over the continuous hatred and bigotry experienced by all people around the globe.

The truth is that there is a fine line between remembering and honoring the past, and living as if we are still at war, about to be hunted and attacked. There is a difference between being cautious and being paranoid. And there is a vast schism between connecting and appreciating Jewish accomplishments and living in fear that the curtain will drop any minute. I believe that we, the Jewish community as a whole, must teach our children to honor our heritage, to support a strong Israel and Jewish communities, and encourage leadership that embraces Jewish unity, positive relationships with our neighbors and world unity.

Letting go of the paranoia and fear will allow us to have an honest relationship with each other and an authentic relationship with God.

ELEVEN

Returning Home

"Return us, Adonai (God), to you and we will return."
Lamentations 5:21

At about 8 a.m. one July morning in 2010, I went for my daily visit to Brentwood Nursing Home and I immediately saw that my father was unresponsive, swollen with fluids and struggling to breathe. I followed the ambulance to Highland Park Hospital and watched as he was placed on a respirator. A nurse hooked up medication through an IV to reduce his dangerously high blood pressure. He remained comatose on the hospital bed in the ICU for an entire week.

A week later, as I stood outside his room while putting on the hospital cover-up, plastic gloves and face mask, I overheard one of the physicians in his room say, "I can't believe he is still alive."

Upset that anyone would speak this way in front of my father, I stormed into the room and interrupted.

"Excuse, me," I snapped, "What is so hard to believe?"

Awkwardly the doctor replied, "I am surprised that he's still alive because most people in his condition would have passed away by now."

"Well, he hasn't," I retorted, "my father is a Holocaust survivor; he went through hell living in the forests for several years."

The physician responded, "Well, that certainly explains everything." He didn't apologize at all, so I dismissed him from my thoughts and went to stand by my father's bed.

The medical staff and I convened shortly after, and the doctors slowly weaned him off the ventilator that afternoon. He was still clinging to life. Over the previous few months he had lost so much weight that his shoulder bones and ribs protruded from his body. His hands and feet appeared twice as large since they were swollen with edema. His arms were black and blue from the IV needles and his face seemed tense and angry. I thought that if anyone can reawaken and emerge from this unconscious state, it would be my father. He had cheated death in the past and, I thought, he could do it again. He is a survivor! He will pull through once more.

The next morning, I returned to the ICU. The lights in his room were dimmed and the curtains drawn. The machines hummed and beeped while monitoring his heart and pulse. I stood at his side and wondered if he somehow managed to speak to me one last time, what would he say?

I was dreaming he would say he was proud to have me as his daughter and proud of all my accomplishments. I hoped he would finally kvell over his grandchildren. Maybe he would even apologize for the hurt and harm he caused our family and would ask me for forgiveness. I even imagined that just maybe on his death bed he would utter the words "I love you".

Or with the realization that his life was ending, he would panic, tremble and be filled with terror. He might even admit that he was scared of dying. But more likely he might say, "Karen, the world is out to get you and the rest of the Jews. Hitler tried to exterminate our people; don't let your children marry non-Jews. Don't finish off what he started. Watch my money very carefully. People will want it, expect it, and try to take it from you. I am warning you, do not disappoint me or your people."

As I stood by his bedside, I recalled speaking intimately with my mother during the weeks leading up to her death. We hugged and cried and then when she lost movement in her limbs, I curled up next to her in bed. She told me that she loved me and would miss watching her beautiful grandchildren grow up. One day I asked her, "Do you believe in the afterlife?"

"I don't know," she said.

"I don't know either, but, if there is life after death, then I am certain that you will be watching over my children and me," I said.

I remember telling my mother that I loved her and would forever miss her. She asked me to promise her one thing, "Don't forget Howard's children. They are still my grandchildren and give them the money that is owed to them."

"I promise," I said.

She said that she wished she could have had a relationship with Howard's children, but the rift was too deep. I recognized that this was one of the deepest regrets of her life. She had wanted her family to get along but it was never going to happen between my father and Helene. And now it was his turn, and I was standing next to his bed.

Gently, I rubbed my father's forehead, brushing aside his hair. I held his hand and looked at his face and began speaking to him. I wasn't sure if he could hear me, but I read that hearing is usually the last sense to deteriorate when people are dying. His nurse thought otherwise and suggested to me that he was most likely incoherent. I paid no attention to her and kept talking.

"Daddy, it is time now for you to return home. God is waiting for you. Let go of all this suffering and pain. Your mother, Beila, and your father, Chaim Shlomo, are waiting for you. Chaya, Leah, Joshpe, and Yehuda Leizer are there, too. Let go, Daddy. You have endured too much suffering in your life. Free yourself from this pain. Just let go," I said softly.

My eyes swelled up with tears that trickled down my cheeks and dropped onto his bed sheets.

"Daddy, I forgive you," I said, "I want you to know that I forgive you."

Compassion filled my heart at that moment. I stood there and repeatedly whispered quietly to him, "I forgive you... I forgive you... I forgive you...."

Suddenly, his eyes popped wide open! I was startled and jumped away. Were my eyes deceiving me? I wiped my tears and saw that he stared right at me. My heart pounded. I moved slightly to the left and his eyes followed me. Then I moved to the right, and his eyes tracked me again. Chills went up and down my spine. I ran out of the room and screamed for the nurse to check him. When I returned with the nurse to the room, his eyes were closed once again. He was transferred to the palliative care treatment center that afternoon and I went to pick up Beba in the city so she could visit him that evening. The following morning, July 29, 2010, he died. I always wondered if he was trying to respond to me in that instant when he looked at me. I'll never know what he was thinking but it didn't matter because I truly forgave him.

It was extraordinary difficult to feel compassion and forgiveness toward my father, a man who caused immeasurable harm to my entire family. I was damaged, and carried the anger and fear until then. Letting go of these bitter emotions allowed me to finally find peace.

Many of us knowingly or unknowingly choose to live with pain from our past. Repeatedly, like a broken record, we continue to feel the devastation over and over again, even though the perpetrator has ended the torment or has disappeared. When we live with these wounds, we are not living in the moment or appreciating life. We are wounded survivors. I didn't want to merely survive; I wanted to be happy, live a meaningful life and make the world a better place.

Compassion is a feeling of deep sympathy and sorrow for those suffering and a desire to alleviate it. The Hebrew word for compassion is rachamim, which is derived from the root word rechem meaning "womb." The mother's compassion begins to develop as the life inside her womb grows.

I think my father lost his ability to feel compassion during the hour he watched his mother and sisters tortured and killed while he hid. People lose their ability to feel all kinds of emotions for all kinds of reasons. I might have continued my father's legacy, but I decided to be the kind of person who cares about the suffering of others. I wanted to make sense of our relationship and my life.

There are many who assume that forgiving automatically means forgetting, but as the philosopher George Santayana said, "Those who do not remember history are condemned to repeat it." I am not suggesting that any of us forget the past, but that we must acknowledge our pain, process our emotions and let it all go. While my father was in the nursing home during the last year of his life, I began to face up to the horrors of my childhood. I finally let my true feelings surface, and allowed myself to remember even the worst moments. My crying usually occurred in the shower and my wails were drowned out by the sounds of the jets spraying the water; these were cathartic moments for me and as quickly as the flood of tears billowed from my eyes, they were washed away. I mourned over never having a healthy and loving relationship with my father. Eventually, when there were no more tears to shed, I realized it was time to forgive my father, to finally seal the wounds of my past, and to let it all go.

Ironically, it is the victim who usually holds onto the pain by remembering and reliving every sordid experience without the goal of moving on. This self-created suffering keeps victims stuck in their dysfunction, and the pain continues. I have not forgotten my past, but I refuse to let it define me.

My father taught me to never trust the world, always watch my back, and never forgive our enemies. Yet, if I adhered to his philosophy, I would have never forgiven him. I, too, would have suffered for the rest of my life. I was ready and willing to free myself from all of this pain and madness.

Immediately following my father's funeral service, we all drove to the cemetery plot for the burial service; the rabbi recited the final prayers. As I stood alongside my father's excavated grave, I glanced inside the hollowed earth and saw a modest looking pinewood coffin resting inside. A sense of calm overcame me and I felt reaffirmed in my decision to have forgiven him. As I shoveled the dirt over his coffin, I knew that I buried the pain, suffering and victimization along with my father.

Barry, however, has not been able to forgive our father and often brings up cutting reminders of his childhood. Following the burial, he vented, "Karen, while I shoveled the dirt onto the grave, I wanted to take the pail and shovel and throw it at the coffin! I hate his miserable soul and hope he ends up in hell!" I remember wishing that Barry had been ready to forgive our father.

To this day, my brother continues to be tormented by his childhood. His wounds have not healed. The anger and hatred live freshly within him as if my father had just recently physically or emotionally abused him. When I try to help him or bring up the topic of forgiveness, he ignores me or changes the subject. I get the feeling that he thinks holding onto his anger somehow punishes our father.

I have noticed that some people believe they can injure and castigate their perpetrators by fighting against forgiveness. They believe that their abusers don't deserve forgiveness and continue to harbor the anger and resentment inside. Sometimes they hold fast to their anger, believing that it is powerful enough to destroy their perpetrators. Yet, ultimately, they are the ones who suffer by absorbing these toxic feelings. Often physical and mental symptoms appear such as depression, anxiety, lack of purpose or unhealthy relationships.

The Hebrew word for forgiveness is teshuvah, which is derived from the root word meaning "return." One can return home to a natural, peaceful state of mind and restore the balance of their relationship with God and their fellow human beings by the act of forgiveness.

I learned from my Jewish day school education that if a Jew has committed a sin against God, then he/she must ask forgiveness directly from God. There are no intermediaries involved since every Jew is personally responsible to atone for his/her own transgressions. To atone for sins against another person, a Jew is obligated to seek forgiveness directly from that person.[4] Unless I ask for forgiveness, I cannot be forgiven. But what about the one who waits a lifetime for that request to forgive and it never comes? What about the victim's need to heal and move on? I had no desire to remain hostage to a lifetime of emotional pain; I needed to forgive without being asked.

On the last day of Passover in April 2011, I went to synagogue to recite Yizkor, the memorial prayer for my father, mother and brother. That morning the rabbi sermonized about the significance of the Israelites taking Joseph's bones from Egypt and bringing them into the land of Canaan for burial. While the Israelites wandered forty years in the desert, Joseph's bones were treated with utmost respect as they were carried alongside the Holy Ark of the Covenant which contained the Ten Commandments. Once the Israelites conquered Canaan, Joseph's bones were finally laid to rest. What made Joseph so laudable? The rabbi stated that Joseph was commended for forgiving his ten half-brothers. When

---

4 *If someone seeks forgiveness three times and is denied, then he/she is exonerated from asking for forgiveness and the onus falls on the person who has refused to forgive.

Joseph was seventeen years old, some of his brothers planned to murder him. They temporarily threw him into a pit and eventually sold him to passing traders on route to Egypt. They soaked Joseph's cloak with animal blood, showed it to their father Jacob, and reported that Joseph was dead. Despite almost dying in the pit, being sold into slavery, and having been imprisoned in Egypt on false charges, Joseph became the most powerful and influential man under the Pharaoh. He became a fully assimilated Egyptian, married an Egyptian woman and raised his two sons. By then the region was plagued with famine and Jacob sent ten of his sons, except for Benjamin, Joseph's full and younger brother, into Egypt to purchase grain. They all met Joseph but did not recognize him. Joseph accused his brothers of spying and put them in jail for a few nights while he spied on them. Eventually, Joseph released them but kept one brother hostage until they brought Benjamin to Egypt. In the very end of this story, Joseph releases both his brothers and all his anger toward them. He had the power to seek revenge, imprison them for a lifetime or even kill them. After Joseph revealed his true identity to his brothers, he said, "I am Joseph, your brother, whom you sold into Egypt. Don't be grieved or angry with yourselves that you sold me, for God sent me before you to preserve life, to give you food, and save you for a great deliverance." Genesis 45:3-15

Then he kisses his brothers and cries. Later, when their father Jacob died, the brothers were still worried that Joseph may harm them, and they sent him a note. Joseph reiterated, "You meant evil against me, but God made it turn out well, that many lives could be saved. Don't be afraid, I will keep you and your little ones alive." Genesis 50:19-21

The Torah never described the brothers openly apologizing or seeking forgiveness from Joseph, yet by his own volition, Joseph forgave them. Joseph never forgot the abuse he incurred from his brothers and candidly acknowledged their evil conduct. If he had excused their actions, there would have been no need to pardon them. He replaced his anger with love. It was because of this exemplary behavior that he merited having his bones brought out of Egypt.

Joseph also recognized God's choreographed presence in his life. He endured the malevolent acts of his brothers and the painful and arduous years living in Egypt abandoned by his family; he hungered to be with his younger brother and his father and he suffered tremendously. On a personal level, maybe Joseph needed to learn the tough lesson of forgiveness. On a collective familial level, he sensed that he rose to a significant and strategic position of authority in Egypt in order to ultimately save his family from the drought. Just imagine, if Joseph had not forgiven his brothers, the twelve tribes of Israel might have vanished.

Several years back, just prior to my son Noah's bar-mitzvah in September of 2005, I was ready to sever all ties with my father. I was tired of hearing his constant insulting remarks about my way of life; I couldn't handle his cursing and negativity anymore. So I excluded him from Noah's bar-mitzvah pictures and I didn't care if he attended the service. Just as Jacob tore his garments as a sign of mourning, after he saw the bloodstained cloak of Joseph, I was ready to become estranged from my father and finally mourn the loss of relationship. Our dysfunctional, miserable relationship needed to end, and I wanted him to physically disappear from my life.

I had longed for a loving father but instead got an angry, hurtful father who never admitted guilt for the way he treated any of us, or displayed any sense of remorse. He never acknowledged any of his wrongdoings and his behavior remained unchanged to the end, but I nevertheless chose to forgive him. I'm quite certain that if my father were alive today and had the opportunity to curse and insult me, he probably would. But since he died, it was my choice to forgive him, because had I not chosen to forgive him, I would be the one suffering and unable to heal and move forward in life. Hadn't I already suffered enough while he was alive? Sometimes I think that the reason my father survived the war, married my mother, and acted the way he did was just so that I would learn about forgiveness. Maybe that's why I'm drawn to the story of Joseph; I admire Joseph's ability to forgive.

TWELVE

An Unexpected Journey

In spite of everything I still believe that people are really good at heart. I simply can't build up my hopes on a foundation consisting of confusion, misery and death.
-Anne Frank

When I asked Holocaust survivors or their children if they could ever forgive the Nazis, they unequivocally and boldly retorted, "Never!" Other Jewish friends said, "Karen, be careful what you write about in your book. Forgiveness sounds too Jesus-like. It is a Christian concept. You will turn off the Jewish community."

"I have yet to forgive the Babylonians!" another friend responded.

"The Babylonians? That was over twenty-five hundred years ago!" I laughed. Some grudges never seem to go away, I thought.

Throughout all my years of Hebrew day school education, the subject of forgiving those involved in the atrocities of the Holocaust was never discussed. That would have been deemed utterly absurd. Elie Wiesel once said that certain people have gone beyond the capacity of being forgiven-- and they do not deserve forgiveness. He once said in a prayer, "God of mercy, have no mercy on these souls who murdered our children; out of compassion, have no compassion for those who have killed our children."

On Holocaust Memorial Day in 2000, the Bundestag invited Wiesel to address the members of its German parliament. In front of the parliament, Wiesel said that though Germany had offered reparations to the Jews and assistance to Israel after the war, there was one thing that Germany had not yet done. The Germans had failed to ask the Jewish people for forgiveness. Within a few weeks of his speech, the chancellor of Germany traveled to Jerusalem and addressed the Knesset, the Israeli parliament. Though some members of the Knesset walked out before he began, the president, on behalf of his generation of Germans, asked the Jewish nation for forgiveness.

Must we have waited over a half of a century remaining embittered and angry toward Germany until they sought forgiveness from us? It certainly would be much easier to forgive our enemies when they ask us— but is it necessary?

If I could face the perpetrators of the Holocaust today, would I be able to forgive them? Seventy years have passed since my father's family was butchered and I wonder if any of the murderers are still alive. What about the Poles who just stood by and witnessed the atrocities? Are they guilty in the same way? Can—or should—they be forgiven, too? Should I also hold grudges against and blame the children of the oppressors? My father had died six months ago and I was preoccupied with these thoughts, but I had no definitive answers.

As long as I could remember, my father had always anticipated returning to Poland. At first he seriously considered traveling with Howard but when Howard died, my father contemplated traveling with Barry. He also suggested to his mistress that they travel there, but nothing ever came of it.

In early March 2011, Bobby's cousins invited us to travel to Italy and stay in a cottage in Tuscany with them; but that trip never materialized. It did, however, give us the impetus to start thinking about taking a vacation abroad. Bobby and I love to travel together and have taken trips to New York, California and Florida, and we have flown to Jamaica and Mexico during the winter holidays.

Recently, Barry returned from a trip to Israel and encouraged me to visit. The first time I traveled to Israel, I was fifteen and spent six weeks touring the country with my youth group. During the weekends I visited with my Aunt Tova and Uncle Chaim at their apartment in Rishon LeTzion. In college, the Jewish Federation of Chicago sent me with three other college student interns to Amishav, a poor neighborhood of Petach Tikvah, just east of Tel-Aviv. I was a camp counselor and tutored English. I stayed on in Israel and spent my junior year abroad at Hebrew University in Jerusalem. Since then I had visited Israel twice, once with Howard and once with my ex-husband. But it had been about twenty-five years since I had last been there, and I decided that it was time to return. So I approached Bobby and asked him,

"Bobby, do you love me?"

"Of course I do," he said, wondering what was coming next.

"Would you do anything for me? "I asked tenderly while batting my brown eyes.

"Of course I would—you know that." Then he knew what was coming.

"I want to go to Israel, and I want you to come with me," I said. "Neither one of us has been there in decades. It's about time we revisit."

"Okay, on one condition," he said. "I want to do a stopover in Europe."

"Of course," I said excitedly and threw my arms around him and kissed him. "You choose the city."

Stopovers in Istanbul and Warsaw proved to work best with our schedules and finances, and he chose Warsaw, with the option to travel to Cracow, the hippest new city in Eastern Europe. The writing was on the wall, I thought. I knew that I was destined to travel to Poland and would be compelled to see my father's hometown of Rajgród.

There was a lot of preparation involved. My father had numerous files on Poland that contained genealogical records, maps, letters, and historical information - all of which I needed to review.

It was imperative that I speak with my first cousin Avi Tzur, my father's nephew. He is the quintessential sabra: born in 1950, two years after the birth of the state of Israel; he was raised in Rishon LeTzion, a town situated east of Tel-Aviv. He is confident, bold, fearless—the very symbol of the modern-day Israeli Jew. He served in the Israel Defense Forces (IDF) as a captain and platoon commander in the Yom Kippur

War. He studied at the Israel Institute of Technology (Technion) in the field of materials engineering and received his M.B.A. from INSEAD in Fontainebleu, France. Since he speaks five languages, he went to work for Motorola operations in its South America division. Avi raised two sons in Israel, both of whom have also served in the IDF. He lives and works in Brazil half of the year, and then he travels back home to Israel. Over the years, he would always ask my father about Poland. Since Avi traveled to Rajgród in 1990, I knew he would have some additional information for me.

"It has been quite some time since we last talked," Avi said. "I haven't seen you since my nephew's wedding in Scottsdale several years ago."

"Tell me," I said, "is it the computer screen making you look so young?" We were Skyping.

Avi smiled. After exchanging some more pleasantries, we talked about his trip to Poland.

"Before I left for Poland in 1990," said Avi, "your father wanted to join me. He wanted me to obtain a personal letter from Lech Walesa, president of Poland, that would ensure his safety there. Underneath his tough exterior, he was a frightened man."

"What did you tell him?" I asked.

"I told him that it was inconceivable to get a letter from the government. Maybe that's why he never went. But he drafted a map of Rajgród, the location of the synagogues, the mikvah (a ritual bath house), the cemetery, and our grandmother's house and farm. He also gave me some names of townspeople, including the names of the two killers who took part in murdering our grandmother and aunts. Their names were Kordash and Jablonski."

"Did your mother provide you with any details?" I asked. "Did she remember anything about Rajgród?"

"Karen, my parents were still alive when I first went to Poland, and they refused to have anything to do with my experience. They did not accept any of my findings and did not cooperate with me. They were emotionally distant."

Avi continued: "Your father had one request from me when I returned to Poland."

"What was it?" I asked.

"He said, 'Avi, you have been a soldier in the IDF and have learned to defend, fight, and kill. Find those Ukrainians and Poles who murdered our family and kill them! Go to my mother's house and take whatever may be left of our family's relics. See if you can get back the house and the farmhouse. It belongs to our family.'"

All of these years I had never considered how my father felt about returning to Poland. So I was taken aback by Avi's comments, but they did seem consistent with my father's way of thinking.

"What did you tell him?" I asked.

"I told him I wasn't going there to kill anyone, but I would confront the killers and let them know that I am the grandson of the woman they killed."

Avi went on: "So I left for Poland in 1990 with just your father's drawing of the shtetl. He had an extraordinary memory of the layout of the town. The map was very accurate except that he was off by a ninety-degree angle. Once I figured that out, everything fell into place."

"So what happened when you went to Rajgród?" I asked.

Avi said that he hired a female Polish interpreter to drive him to Rajgród. He went to my grandmother's house with the police, and asked if he could just come in and see if there were any household remnants from his grandmother. That is all he wanted—nothing more.

"Who answered the door?" I asked.

"An elderly women was living there. She said that she owned the property. She was afraid that I was going to confiscate her home."

"Where were the killers?" I asked.

"Kordash took over our grandmother's home in 1941 but both he and Jablonski were killed in 1946 by the Polish Resistance. I learned that the Russians first invaded Rajgród from April to September in 1940 and set up a cultural center in town. The Jews cooperated with the Russians back then. Jablonski arranged an attack on the center and threw two grenades killing one Russian soldier and four Jewish women. Then the Russian secret service rounded up sixty non-Jewish Poles and a Catholic priest and killed them all. Jablonski continued to terrorize the Russians and Jews and welcomed the Nazis as they entered the town. In 1946, the Polish resistance came through Rajgród, and searched for anyone who had collaborated with the Germans during the war. Jablonski was killed, but I don't have the details."

"What about Kordash? How was he killed?" I asked.

"One day Kordash went with another neighbor named Karpatski into the forests to chop down trees and collect wood on their wagons. Karpatski left the woods and returned back to Rajgród a bit earlier. Just a half hour later, Kordash's wagon came rolling into town with his blood stained body on top of all the logs. There was a bayonet thrusted into the center of his chest."

What goes around comes around, I thought.

"I found out that the head of the Polish resistance lived near Rajgród and fled to America fearing revenge from the Kordash family. He finally returned in the 1970s to a town between Rajgród and Gdnask," he continued.

Avi also said that Kordash's sister and her family lived around the block from our grandmother's home.

"Who lives in our grandmother's house today?" I asked.

Avi did not know. He said that he also contacted a lawyer hoping that the land would be returned to our family. "The Polish government was not cooperating, nor giving us the money for the value of the land back then," he said.

He also explained that he located the cemetery at the edge of town in accordance with my father's drawing.

"There were no markers," Avi said, "and no one could see that a cemetery existed there—just deserted forests. Three feet of dead, dried-up leaves covered the tombstones. I started clearing away some of the leaves and found a grave, but it was Shabbat that day, and I stopped. So I took a picture of the gravestone and left. Our grandmother also owned a summer ranch and farm at the edge of town, and I met with a neighbor across the road who verified that our grandmother owned the land."

Avi said that he would scan and forward all of his information so I could take it along to Rajgród. He emailed pictures of the town, our grandmother's home, the cemetery and town square and wished me a safe journey.

Just six weeks later, Bobby and I boarded a LOT Airliner and headed to Warsaw. Whenever I have traveled abroad, I had always felt the need to hide my Jewish identity because of my fears of being singled out and attacked. My friend Lisa, a child of a survivor, said that whenever she traveled, she never ordered the kosher meals on the plane. She was afraid to let anyone know that she was Jewish. But this time was different. This time I was not going to cave in to my fears. I boldly and proudly wore my gold Jewish star pendant around my neck. Many family members and friends warned me to be careful in Poland.

"Anti-Semitism still exists there," they said. "Don't be naive. Don't go knocking on the Polish people's doors demanding that your family property be returned. Be very careful."

Bobby said, "Karen, you are an anomaly. You are afraid of bugs and spiders and need me to always walk you into your home at night to make sure the house is safe. Yet, you are willing to travel to Poland and openly display your Jewish identity."

We landed in the capital city of Warsaw and immediately took a three-and-a-half-hour express train to Cracow. Sitting inside the cabin and peering out the window, I looked at Poland's vast countryside. The land was luscious green from the early spring rains, and the farms and forests sprawled out between the towns. Many of the farms were very old and neglected, but some were newly constructed. Groves of thin, erect pine trees reached toward the sky; they were intermingled with lengthy, beautiful, white birch trees thrusting upward and competing for the sunlight; these forests were magnificent and serene. Yet I focused on these forests as places of sheer hell—fear and then death—for the Jews during World War II. My father had lived in these forests night after night, week after week, season after season, hunted like a wild animal by the Nazi predators.

In the southern region of Poland, situated on the Vistula River and near the Carpathian Mountains, lies the magnificent ancient capital, Cracow. It was once the leading academic and cultural center of Poland, and it has retained its old-world charm because it had sustained neglible bombing during World War II. We stayed at the Hotel Pollera in the Old Quarter of the city. I learned that the Germans had occupied this once-famous hotel during the war. When Cracow was liberated, Pollera was used as the headquarters for the Russian army. As we settled into our room, I imagined this hotel swarming with German soldiers years ago.

I shuddered at the thought of the Nazis sleeping in these rooms, eating, drinking and smoking in the dining room, and strategizing their military operations.

In Cracow we visited the Old Jewish district, Kazimierz, which was once a prominent and wealthy Jewish community that retained its own jurisdiction and culture. A few synagogues have remained, along with a Jewish cemetery that dates back to the 1500s. Roughly sixty thousand Jews were confined to the Cracow ghetto—and eventually were annihilated. Nearby, off the bank of the river, in a gloomy industrial neighborhood, we toured Oskar Schindler's factory and museum. This German businessman saved over one thousand Jews by employing them at his factory.

Our plans to visit Auschwitz-Birkenau on our very last day in Cracow changed when we learned that it would be closed due to a special "March of the Living" ceremony. But in a last-minute attempt, we managed to book a tour and headed to Auschwitz-Birkkenau; it was Sunday afternoon, May 1, 2011, which coincidentally was Yom Ha Shoah (Holocaust Memorial Day). There are many concentration camps to consider visiting in Poland, but we chose Auschwitz because Bobby's father had been deported there. Auschwitz is synonymous with the Holocaust and is one of the most well-known concentration camps in all of Europe. It is located forty miles west of Cracow, adjacent to the town of Oswiecim.

It was a cold and dreary spring day with intermittent heavy showers. I wore three layers of socks and clothes and carried an umbrella in an unsuccessful attempt to stay warm and dry. It was encouraging to observe that the majority of those on our tour bus to the death camp were Poles, Europeans, and other world travelers from college age to seniors. During our hour ride, we watched a chilling documentary on the liberation of this extermination camp by the Russian soldiers, their first encounters with the survivors, and the personal testimonies of survivors. As we approached the prison camp area, I noticed that the town of Oswiecim had newly built homes. Why would anyone want to live next door to one of the most hellish places on earth?

When I was in grade school, I remember reading books about Jewish families forced into cattle cars and sent off to the nearest concentration camps to be gassed to death. Pictures of emaciated Jews wearing striped clothing and standing behind the barbed wire fences of concentration camps, looking like the living dead, left imprints in my mind.

Concentration camps terrified me. Soon I was about to walk on one of the largest mass murder sites of mankind and I started to tremble.

As our tour bus pulled into the parking lot, I began to weep.

"Bobby," I said, "I am not sure I can handle the tour. Maybe I just need to stay on the bus."

"Do what you think is necessary," he said as he held me.

After calming down, I mustered up all my energy, held his hand, and walked off the bus. The very first thing I noticed were massive crowds of young Jewish teenagers from Canada's "March of the Living." I felt somewhat relieved to see all these young, vibrant Jewish teens; the next generation of our people, I thought, will certainly not forget.

We slowly followed our tour guide, a Polish woman with an appropriately grave disposition. As our tour walked toward the front gate entrance of the camp, I was immediately struck by the cynical message on the infamous iron gate sign, Arbeit macht frei (work makes you free). As I walked underneath the sign, chills went up and down my spine. As soon as we entered the concentration camp, we saw neatly arranged rows of barracks that once housed thousands of prisoners. We walked toward Block 11, a barrack that contained prison cells where countless victims were methodically tortured to death. The Polish prisoners were the first to be used as guinea pigs and gassed in these cells. Together our group walked downward through the narrow dark hallways of the prison, deep into the bowels of the barracks. I started to hyperventilate. I needed air and needed to quickly escape from this hell-hole. Dashing past the long lines of people walking down through the cramped space, I pushed my way upward, climbing the twisted staircase until I reached the top. I raced outside the barrack. Catching my breath in the damp cold air was a relief, and my breathing slowly got back to normal. As I became more focused, I realized that I was standing just a few feet away from a once electrified barbed-wire fence and near one of the many tall wooden guard towers that surrounded the perimeter of the entire camp. Suddenly, the ominous clouds burst open and the rain poured down on me. Chilled and drenched, I still opted to wait outside in the damp cold for everyone to emerge from inside the barracks.

Next, our group entered another building in which piles of shoes, luggage, eyeglasses, and human hair were exhibited in different rooms. These were the prisoners' personal belongings which were stripped from them as they arrived at the camp. Looking at the tons of human hair stirred me again, and I broke down and wept. I quickly walked over to an open window of the barracks to breathe in some cold misty air before I could continue on with the tour.

We left this area and slowly walked toward the building that contained the gas chambers. Claustrophobia once again engulfed me as I stood with the group inside the chamber; it was dim and eerie and the walls were gray, grim and cracked. The only small opening was from above, where the Cyclon B poisonous gas pellets dropped down into the room suffocating everyone. As the Jews gasped for air, they climbed upward over the dead bodies and formed a pyramid that reached upward to the ceiling of the chamber. Others banged on the doors, but their end was inexorable: they all suffocated to death.

Desperately needing to exit this chamber, I ran off into the next room and left everyone behind. I stopped cold as I stared at the crematoriums. Jewish prisoners would be forced to drag the naked bodies that had been gassed into these ovens to be turned into a pile of ashes. I fled outside and stood under the open skies. Soon my breathing returned to normal.

We left Auschwitz and drove along the train tracks just a few minutes down the road to Birkenau, an adjacent camp that was built to expedite the murder of Jews. Nothing has changed at this ghastly place; it remains untouched from seventy years ago. We walked in the footsteps of the Jews on those infamous train tracks to where the dreaded selections of the prisoners were carried out as the gas chambers and crematorium lay in wait for them in the distance. Six thousand Jews were gassed each day in this vast, ghostly camp. Distancing ourselves from the tour, Bobby and I stood near the barbed-wire fence and recited the mourners' kaddish. I prayed for all the souls who had died here, and prayed that they were resting in peace.

At the end of the tour, I approached the tour guide and asked her why there were neighborhoods built so close to this concentration camp. She explained that when the Nazis built Auschwitz-Birkenau, they needed more bricks for the crematoriums and barracks, as well as homes for the SS officers. They also wanted to completely isolate Auschwitz from the public, so they forcibly evicted the non-Jewish Poles from their homes in the surrounding towns; they gave them twenty minutes to leave or be killed. When the war ended, the Poles from those towns returned to their property and rebuilt their homes.

I told the guide that her job was a very honorable one, and I commended her for her sincere efforts to convey the graphic information about the camps to the world.

We returned to Cracow and strolled through the quaint old quarter of the city walking through the largest medieval town square in all of Europe. There was a week full of celebrations in the square in honor of the beatification of Pope John Paul II. Crowds of people attended the open-air concerts, exhibitions, and slide shows commemorating the life of the pontiff. That evening marked the culmination of events, and thousands of Poles crowded the old city square. In 1978, the Polish-born archbishop of Cracow had been elevated to the papacy, bringing great pride to this country, since he was first Slavic (indeed, the first non-Italian) pope in 455 years.

I recalled that in college I wrote a term paper on the silence of the Papacy during World War II. Pope Pius XII had a position of power and influence in the world, yet failed to use his status to publicly denounce and condemn the mass murders of the Jews and minorities under the Nazi regime. Pope John Paul II, on the other hand, became an inspirational leader to the world and breached the two-thousand-year history of turbulence and pain between the Catholics and Jews. He was the first pope to enter a synagogue, to publicly denounce anti-Semitism, to recognize the state of Israel, and to visit Yad Vashem, the National Holocaust Memorial in Jerusalem. Coincidentally, his beatification ceremony was held on May 1, 2011, Holocaust Memorial Day. We joined in with the people of Cracow and admiringly watched the festivities of the final evening on the square.

The next morning we returned to bustling Warsaw. By the onset of World War II, Warsaw was home to over three hundred and fifty thousand Jews, which was the second-largest population center of Jews at that time (second only to New York City). In November 1940 the Nazis set up the Warsaw Ghetto, the largest of its kind, by building brick walls topped with barbed wire, with armed guards stationed on the outer perimeter of the walls. All the Jews of Warsaw were barricaded inside and closed off from the outside world. By June 1942, those who had survived the ghetto's deplorable conditions of starvation and rampant diseases were deported to the Treblinka extermination camp. Approximately three hundred Jews survived by the time the ghetto was liberated in January 1945.

Bobby and I visited the remnant of the ghetto wall, which was inconspicuously located in an inner courtyard of apartment buildings. Adjacent to the wall, in a basement apartment, was a small museum providing us with the historic details of the ghetto and the uprising of the Jews. There was a plaque and some candles inserted into a hole in the ghetto wall and flowers planted in rectangular planters on the side.

When the Nazis invaded Warsaw, they demolished over 80 percent of the buildings, so after the war was over, the Poles painstakingly restored the Old Town based on old photographs and paintings. We spent hours strolling through the streets of this historic Old Town, a quaint and picturesque area of Warsaw that had retained its medieval architecture. The Old Town square market is lined with colorful buildings, shops, and cafes; artists and vendors display their wares, and street performers entertain the children.

We bought some lody (ice cream) and walked toward the rows of artists to view their paintings. There were contemporary and traditional drawings of the old city of Warsaw and of the countryside of Poland. Then I suddenly noticed that there were several paintings grouped together that depicted observant Jews. I walked closer to the pictures and stared at them. Each picture was of an older Jewish man with a long beard. Some of the men had their heads covered with a kippah or tefillin (phylacteries) which are worn during weekday prayers. Some men wore the tallit (prayer shawl), and all of them were sitting at a table—either at home or in the synagogue—holding coins. Near them on the table was an opened money pouch, and they were all counting their money.

"Bobby," I called, "come here and take a look at these drawings. What do you make of them?"

Bobby's immediate response was: "This is flagrant anti-Semitism. It doesn't surprise me that they have these pictures displayed openly in the heart of this city!"

"Wait a second, Bobby," I said. "Don't come to conclusions so readily. Take a look at their faces. They don't appear scheming or demonic. Just expressionless. I'm not sure what to make of this artwork."

So I walked across the square and asked a young artist to tell me more about these pictures.

"These pictures are good luck charms," she said in broken English.

I was puzzled by her response and asked, "What do you mean?"

"We hope they will bring us money," she said. "Many Poles have these pictures in their homes. Some hang them upside down in hopes that money will easily drop out of the pouch."

Bobby didn't believe a word she said and so I took some photos of the artwork and we left the square.

While we were returning home from Warsaw to the United States, a man on the plane called out my name. I turned and saw Radoslaw, my hair dresser's husband who was born and raised in Bialystok. They live minutes from my home. He is a coin collector and travels to Poland monthly.

"Oh my goodness, I never imagined I would bump into anyone that I knew on LOT airlines," I said.

"How was your trip to Poland?" he asked.

"It was very good. And you?" I asked.

"I had my usual business in Bialystok and visited with family and friends there," he said.

"Rado, something is puzzling me and I want to hear your thoughts," I said.

So I pulled out my camera and showed him those portraits of the Jews counting their money. "Can you explain these pictures? I asked.

"Karen, you know that I am a coin collector--and I do a lot of business in Poland."

"Yes, I know, that is exactly why I want your opinion." I said.

"Well, the Polish people see these pictures as a sign of abundance and wealth. They believe it will bring them fortune. In fact, I have several in my home office. Next time you're over, I'll show you them."

"How does this symbolism connect with the Jews?" I asked.

"I have no idea where it originated," he said. "Many Poles give these pictures as gifts to one another, wishing for a prosperous year for their friends and family members."

"You don't find this insulting to the Jews?" I asked.

"Not at all," he said.

Rado did not seem to harbor any animosity toward Jews. The origination of these Jewish images may have casted Jews in an anti-Semitic role but today it seems quite the contrary. In Poland I also noticed pictures of Jews playing in Klezmer bands and holding Torahs. I didn't answer Rado, but I thought about the danger of any kind of stereotyping. Today the pictures bring good fortune, what happens if tomorrow they don't?

The house on the left is my father's home in Rajgród and
the bus station is to the right.

THIRTEEN

The Road to Rajgród

I'm going HOME, back to the place where I belong and where your love has always been enough for me, I'm not running from, no I think you got me all wrong, I don't regret this life I chose for me...."
-Chris Daughtry

Bobby and I continued to wander through the business, residential, and university areas of Warsaw. Soon it started pouring, the wind was howling and our feet were sopping wet. It became unseasonably cold so we rushed back to our hotel in time to watch the snow blanket the city. It felt good to have Bobby with me; I felt protected, cared for and loved as I was beginning to feel nervous and unsettled about the next couple of days.

The following morning we waited in the lobby for Maciej (pronounced Macheck) Martyniuk, our private tour guide, to take us through northeastern Poland for two days. He grabbed our luggage in his van and we began our journey into the countryside of Poland. He was full of enthusiasm and began to provide us with a wealth of historical and cultural information about his homeland.

While driving eastward toward Bialystok, I started to ask him personal questions about his family. Maciej was born in Lublin, southeastern Poland, in 1972, and was married with two children. He was Christian, yet he said that he adhered to many of the biblical commandments of the Torah.

"I do not work on the Sabbath," he said, "beginning with sundown on Friday night until Saturday evening, I stay at home and spend time with my family. We do not eat milk with any meat products—and certainly no pork."

"You observe many of the same laws I did growing up as an Orthodox Jew," I said and was baffled. "Why do you, as a Christian, follow these rules?"

"I am a Seventh Day Adventist and it is part of our religious beliefs."

Maciej also explained that his maternal grandmother, who had encouraged the family to keep these observances, was born a Jew in Dubow, Poland, in 1925. She converted to Christianity and was baptized in 1949.

"Did your grandmother ever discuss her experiences during the Holocaust?" I asked.

"Many of her relatives died," he said, "but she refused to talk about her life during the war. She eventually married a Polish man and had four daughters and one son. My mother was a Seventh Day Adventist, too, and I have continued to follow the traditions of my family."

Remaining in Poland after the war must have been very traumatic for his grandmother, I thought. Over a million children perished during the Holocaust, while tens of thousands were lost and stranded. She was a fugitive in her own country, uprooted from her home and torn away from her family. I sat in the car wondering what might have happened to her during the war. Was she a slave to Nazis in a concentration camp? Since she was close to my father's age at the time of the Nazi invasion, perhaps she went into hiding, like my father, in the forests of Poland? Maybe she survived by hiding in the sewers and tunnels of the major cities? Maciej said that she never returned to her home in Dubow, so perhaps she was cared for in one of the Christian orphanages. Maybe she felt that converting to Christianity would be her only means of survival. Since Seventh Day Adventists follow religious practices that are similar to Jewish observances, it may have seemed like the best alternative for her. On one hand, she was saved and cared for by her Christian neighbors, yet she could never be free and live as a Jew. Her identity had been stripped from her, and her remaining connection to her family and her people had vanished. Sadly, to this very day, she is unable to divulge and unlock the anguish that she has carried for over seventy years; maybe she is still crippled by the trauma of the war. I was sad that her children and the world will never know her story. As we continued our journey deep into the countryside, I wondered how many tens of thousands of Polish people today are descendants of those abandoned Jewish children of the Holocaust.

We stopped for lunch in Tykocin and toured the small village. We learned that in the early 1500s, several Jewish families were invited to settle in this town by Gasztold, a nobleman who owned the land. The Jews eventually became an autonomous community, with a rabbi heading the town council. But during World War II, roughly 1,700 Jews were rounded up and taken to dug-out pits in the nearby Lopuchowo Forest, where they were executed in waves. Though the majority of synagogues throughout Poland were demolished during the war, we were able to visit the seventeenth-century baroque synagogue in Tykocin, still intact because the Nazis had used it as a stable for their animals. There are no Jews for miles in every direction, but the town maintains it as a museum, visited mostly by Jewish tours such as March of the Living.

We left and continued driving eastward toward Bialystok. The green countryside was covered with spots of snow in the shaded terrain from the previous night's snowfall. Every few miles or so, there was a young woman standing on the side of the highway dressed very provocatively. It was cold, too cold for the high heels they were wearing. I wondered what they were doing. Maciej first said they were picking mushrooms, but then explained that these young women came from the poorer neighboring countries and were surviving as prostitutes.

Finally we reached Bialystok, the largest city in northeastern Poland, located on the banks of the Biala River and surrounded by miles of wilderness. By the end of the 1800s, the majority of this city's population had been Jewish, and prior to World War II, there were over 50,000 Jews. My grandmother Beila and her family were part of the community in Bialystok. Beila's mother, Chana Kagan, was born in Janova, a nearby town, in 1860, and she married Avram Aba Fistul from Lithuania. Together they settled in Janova. Beila was born in 1896; she was the middle child of five children: she had two older brothers, Leibel and Yankel, and two younger siblings, Michel and Raizel. When Avram died in 1912, Chana took her children and moved to Bialystok to start a new life.

In Eastern Europe, arranged marriages were common, and Jews from nearby towns would marry one other. In 1913, Beila at the age of seventeen, left her family in Bialystok and moved to Rajgród to marry my grandfather, Chaim Shlomo Szteinsaper, who was thirty-eight years old.

Bialystok was then a major industrial center, and Jews worked in the textile and silk industry and also became shopkeepers, doctors, lawyers, actors, musicians, teachers, and so on. Jewish Bialystokers also pursued an intellectual, cultural, and religious life. Educational institutions, theater, charitable foundations, youth movements, and political organizations all took root in Bialystok. But poverty was also rampant among the Jewish community, and many lived as beggars; some even engaged in criminal activity.

Zionism flourished in the early part of the twentieth century, and many Jews were encouraged to migrate and establish communities in Palestine. Gitel, my father's eldest sister, moved to Bialystok from Rajgród in 1927, and she became involved with the Zionist movement. She studied the Hebrew language, changed her name to Tova, meaning "good" since Gitel means good, too, and eventually emigrated to Palestine with a group of Jews in 1939.

My father shared only one story about his family in Poland before the war. When he was a young boy, his mother, Beila, sent him to Bialystok with food and goods to visit his grandmother, Chana, and his sister Tova, who was seventeen years old at that time. His mother also handed him a hard salami and told him to share it with his sister. As soon as he arrived in Bialystok, Tova grabbed the salami and shared it with her friends, leaving him nothing. My father spoke so bitterly about Tova's actions that maybe this was the incident which prompted him to feel that in life he should always put himself first and not share, not even with his own family. It occurred to me that my father, who was always vigilant about watching his fat and cholesterol intake, had a soft spot for a chunk of hard salami. He never missed the chance to indulge in my special baked salami every Rosh Hashanah and Passover, and he enjoyed eating it all year round.

We visited the original apartment building at 9 Nowy Swiat where my great grandmother Chana had lived with her children; somehow it had miraculously survived the Nazi bombings. This once-impressive four-story edifice towered over all the newer apartments and homes on the block, and was undergoing major renovations. Underneath the sheer white construction cloth that covered the building were intricate artistic patterns etched along the facade and upper soffit of the building. Protruding balconies with wrought-iron enclosures were on the second and fourth levels of this grand structure.

Bobby, Maciej and I continued strolling through the town, which was rebuilt after World War II. A clock tower faced the open square and overshadowed all the buildings. It was originally built in the 1740s by Count Branicki, a Polish nobleman who invited the Jews to settle in Bialystok and provided them with land and granted them equal rights. At the beginning of the 1800s, Jewish merchants owned most of the shops on the square, and by the 1900s the town square flourished with businesses. We drank coffee at a local cafe, shopped in the stores and admired the facades of the decorated brownstones. The Jewish businesses that once lined this area had all disappeared.

Maciej directed me to the records building just off the square to research some genealogical information. While inside the office, a history student overheard my requests for help and without my knowledge began discovering some of my family information. He said that my grandmother's younger siblings, Michel and Raizel Fistul, had lived and owned a home and store across the street from their mother at 10 Nowy Swiat. A synagogue called Nevelt Beth Midrash was located on that block. The area where my grandmother's family lived was once a thriving Jewish neighborhood in Bialystok, just a few short blocks from where we were in the records building. I researched and, with Maciej's help, found documents in Russian belonging to my great grandfather Yankel Szteinsaper, who owned some land.

We left the office with the documents and wandered the streets of Bialystok because Maciej was committed to finding the memorial for the Jews who perished in the Great Synagogue of Bialystok. We eventually discovered the memorial, which was erected in 1995 and was inconspicuously located between a couple of apartment buildings on a side street near the square. The Great Synagogue had been a magnificently designed structure that was built in 1913 and attracted prestigious cantors from Poland and all throughout Europe. During the 1920s and '30s, city and regional officials from Poland celebrated national holidays in this house of worship. On June 27, 1941, the Nazis barricaded approximately two thousand Jews of Bialystok inside the synagogue and torched them alive. All that remains is the large black twisted metal frame from the dome of the synagogue, now resting awkwardly on the ground. Below the frame, carved into the ground, is the shape of a Jewish star made from stones expanding outward from the frame. Behind the dome is a grey stone wall with two dark bronze-colored plaques. One plaque is an illustration of the synagogue as it looked before the war, and the second plaque describes in Polish, Hebrew, and English the horrifying event that occurred on that fateful day. A seven-tiered menorah is perched on top of the wall, silently guarding the remains of this horrendous calamity. Without speaking, Bobby and I searched for pebbles on the ground nearby and placed them next to the metal frame, as we do when we visit a grave.

In the evening, Bobby and I ate at Tokaj, an authentic Hungarian restaurant on the 3rd floor of an apartment building off the square. We listened to two men playing the live Hungarian folk music on their accordions as we ate our meal. Gazing over the streets and rooftops of the buildings, I imagined this city as it lay in dire ruins under the six years of Nazi occupation. Just as Warsaw lay in shambles, Bialystok had been burnt to the ground, leveled to a pile of rubble. My great grandmother Chana, my grandmother Beila's sibling Michel, Raizel, Leibel and their children died during the Nazi invasion: they were rounded up into the Bialystok ghetto and sent off to Treblinka, a nearby concentration camp. Her brother Jankel, however, died in Moscow during the war, and his children died in Treblinka. The entire Jewish community of Bialystok vanished after 1941.

The following morning after a Polish breakfast that included pierogi, sauerkraut, all kinds of smoked fish, stuffed cabbage and rye bread we got back in the van and headed to Rajgród. It is forty-five miles northwest of Bialystok, nestled on picturesque Lake Rajgródzkie. The town has a peninsula curving outward into the lake, and the coastal areas contain several marshes and swamps. This natural wetland is a breeding site for eagles, cranes, nightingales, swans, wild ducks, and other waterfowl, and the freshwater lake contains several species of fish such as pike, perch, whiting, and eel. The lake and town are surrounded by the ancient primeval forests of mostly pine, along with Norwegian spruce and lime trees where woodpeckers, owls and other birds nest. There is a diversity of land animals, such as moose, elk, and wild boar; even the endangered wolves, bison, and lynx can be found roaming in these vast woods. Rajgród's population today is roughly two thousand inhabitants, and it attracts summer tourists from around the area for sailing, boating, fishing, and other water sports.

Driving through the countryside, although it was scenic, I began to ponder why my ancestors settled in these lands. I often hear to this very day that Poland was a very anti-Semitic country, so why did more than 3.3 million Jews gravitate here and why did it become a haven for the world's largest Jewish population?

Weeks later after we'd left Poland, I was still thinking about this question. So I started reading about Poland's history and the migration of the Jews into Poland. As early as the tenth and eleventh centuries, the Baltic people of Lithuania and Latvia retained jurisdiction of the northeastern region of Poland and eventually erected a fortified citadel on Castle Hill at the edge of the peninsula of Rajgród. They had called this strategic stronghold Raj, meaning paradise. Raj was conquered and destroyed by the Teutonic Knights, a crusading military order, who terrorized northern Poland for decades. Battles continued over this region, and by the 1400s, Poland fell back under the Lithuanian duchy and they continued to reign through the 1500s. During the 1600s, the Swedish and Russian empires declared war on these lands, and fighting continued to plague this Polish-Lithuanian commonwealth. In 1795, Poland was partitioned among the kingdoms of Prussia, the Russian Empire, and the Austrian Empire (as Rajgród was near the borders of the Prussian and Russian Empires). In 1831, the Russians made attempts to capture the city of Rajgród and fortify the castle, but they retreated eastward from the Polish uprising forces. By 1918, Poland regained its independence, only to be partitioned by Nazi Germany and the Soviet Union by the beginning of World War II, which was triggered when Germany invaded Poland on September 1, 1939. Following World War II, Poland was under the communist rule of the Soviet Union until 1989.

From the late eleventh century until the late sixteenth century, the Polish kingdom was a safe haven for the persecuted Jewish refugees who fled the pogroms of western Europe. Jewish merchants had arrived on Polish soil as early as the tenth century, and during the first Crusades in 1098, an influx of Jews migrated into the region under Polish royalty. Jews had a positive influence in developing and stabilizing the Polish economy. Mieszko III, the duke of Greater Poland who ruled in the latter part of the twelfth century, minted coins with Hebrew inscriptions on them. In the year 1264, Duke Boleslaus granted a broad range of religious freedoms and trading rights for the Jews and exempted them from enslavement and serfdom. This precedent of official protection for the Jews created by Duke Boleslaus became the foundation of future Jewish prosperity in Poland. Under the royal protection of King Casimir the Great, who reigned in the fourteenth century, Jewish refugees were encouraged to settle in Poland; the state continued to grant them free trade and legal protection. But anti-Semitism again re-emerged as the Black Plague took its toll throughout Europe. Blood libel accusations began to surface, and the first pogroms in Poland began to occur in the latter half of the fourteenth century, especially along the German borders. Jews continued to flee Germany and were welcomed into the Polish Commonwealth.

With the expulsion of the Jews from Spain in 1492, as well as from Germany, Austria, and Hungary in later years, Poland became the destination of many exiled Jews. By the middle of the sixteenth century, Poland had become home to the world's largest Jewish communities; and in 1580, the Jews established the Council of Four Lands, a central body of Jewish self-government in Poland. Polish Jews established cultural centers, schools, and Talmudic centers that became the leading cultural and spiritual centers of the Jewish people.

From 1648 to 1657, the oppressed Cossacks of Ukraine wanted their independence from Poland, and they rebelled against the Commonwealth and the Jews, who collected taxes from their estates. The Cossacks killed hundreds of thousands of Poles and Jews, ending the Polish reign over them, only to be conquered by the tzardom of Russia.

As the Commonwealth weakened, growing religious strife between the Catholics and Protestants emerged, and this caused an environment of religious fervor and a rise in anti-Semitism from the seventeenth century onward. After the partition in 1795 and Poland's destruction as a sovereign state, Polish Jews were subjected to continued anti-Semitism by all three empires: Prussia, Russia and Austria.

Jews are recorded settling in the city of Rajgród as early as 1587, but there was no organized community at that time. The Jews living in Rajgród were hired by the aristocratic landlords to collect rents and taxes from the peasants and to help maintain economic stability in the region. By 1676 there were 131 Jewish residents; by 1719 the Jews of Rajgród had established a community and had built a cemetery, which was located south of town near the village of Opartowo. They had also erected a small wooden synagogue. By 1747, a Chevra Kadisha had been founded: this is a burial society responsible for protecting, cleansing, and dressing the corpses for burial. By 1799 there were 416 Jews living in Rajgród and its neighboring towns, which represented forty-four percent of the general population. Jews began successfully trading ploughs, leather, and fish, and by the 1800s, the Jews were becoming prosperous in Rajgród. By the middle of the 1800s, there were more than 1,600 Jews living in Rajgród, and they made up 86 percent of the general population. The Jews of Rajgród became merchants and owners of shops that sold smoked fish and eel, fabric, clothing, tea, groceries, grain, hardware, soda water, and leather. They were tailors, hatmakers, butchers, bakers, cattle traders, and coachmen.

But by the late nineteenth and early twentieth century, the economy began to deteriorate, and some of the Rajgród Jews left and immigrated to the "golden land" of America and other foreign lands to fulfill their dreams of a better life. By the beginning of World War II, there were roughly seven hundred Jews still living in Rajgród. My father's family lived in a house located at the center of town, facing the central square. His family also owned a farm just a mile south of town, where they grew vegetables and had a few animals and ducks.

How did they end up in Rajgród? I thought about my grandfather, Chaim Shlomo, the son of Yankel Wolf Szteinsaper of Rajgród and Leah Kalecki. My father was able to trace his family's lineage back to the late 1400s, when our ancestors were expelled from Spain.

As we drove along Highway 61, the only route into and out of Rajgród, I looked out the window; perched above the town's rooftops, telephone poles, and specially constructed nest towers were the impressive stork nests that have been in continuous use for hundreds of years. Tall and long-necked white birds with massive wingspans were flying and hovering over their nests feeding their fledglings.

We were greeted by the green-and-white city sign for Rajgród and immediately to our right was a cemetery. The tombstones and graves could be readily seen from the road and seemed to be clustered tightly together. Continuing along Highway 61, we passed several farms and homes for a mile-long stretch—until we reached the center of town. Highway 61 turns into Warsaw Street, the main street of Rajgród, and is roughly five city blocks long. It is lined by many faded brown and grey homes and a few white and beige two-story apartment buildings. A few facades of the older buildings were painted over with inharmonious colors, such as chartreuse, bright orange, and lime yellow; a few stores had signs selling lody (ice cream) and Zywiec beer. Toward the edge of the town was a neo-Gothic-style, red-brick church, built around 1906, that was bigger than every building in town. We parked at Rajrodzki market, the town square, which had a triangle-shaped grass area and park. Lining the square were several nineteenth-century houses. Within the park there were a few drinking fountains, a small pale green water pump, a flagpole, a few benches along the sidewalks, and an old bulletin board with no information on it. Side streets veered in several angles, away from the square, mostly toward the lake.

It was noontime, and traffic was light. A car or truck would pass by every couple of minutes on Warsaw Street, and we saw an occasional pedestrian walking the town's old brown brick sidewalks. Bobby videotaped the surroundings as I walked with Maciej toward the middle of the square.

Facing northward, I noticed the bus station, a small mustard-yellow shack where the bus had pulled up to let out a passenger. Adjacent to the station was a two-story house with a brightly painted pink façade with gray cement sides. This house was located at the corner of Maya and Placa 1000 Lecia Streets. It was my father's childhood home. He was born Avrum Jakov Stzeinsaper and grew up in this house for nineteen years. My heart pounded; and I felt like the moment was surreal. Seventy years had passed, and time was continuing to move forward; yet as I stood here and stared at my father's home, it seemed as though time stood still.

This simply designed home had cement steps leading up to the wooden front door. Windows with painted white panes were on each side of the door, and directly above on the second floor. There were no shrubs or vegetation surrounding the house, only more gray cement. Slowly, Maciej and I walked toward the house, climbed the steps and knocked on the front door. We waited, but no one answered. There was a flimsy wire fence surrounding the house, and we walked around it to the back of the house from the side of the bus station. There was a decrepit outdoor toilet in the back yard of the bus lot, and as we peered into my grandmother's yard, we noticed an old wooden shack that looked to be over a hundred years old. The door was propped open and someone was moving about inside.

"Hello," shouted Maciej in Polish. "Can we talk to you?"

No one came out of the shack. So we waited a few more minutes.

"We would like to chat with you and ask you a few questions about Rajgród," continued Maciej.

Still no answer, and we waited. I noticed a small German Shepherd standing guard near the back entrance of the home, and I motioned it to come toward us hoping that whoever was in the shack might decide to exit. The dog seemed friendly, wagged its tail as it approached us from the other side of the fence. Immediately, we saw a woman leaving the shack, and Majiek again said, "Hello, we have just arrived in Rajgród, can we ask you some questions?"

The woman looked to be in her sixties and she hesitatingly walked toward us. She seemed bothered by us—and uninterested in having a conversation. Maciej said that I had come here from the United States to visit Rajgród, that I was the granddaughter of Beila Szteinsaper, the woman who lived in this house before the war.

"Can we chat with you, possibly come into your home?" asked Maciej. The woman rushed to the dog and barely looked at us. She quietly said, "No, you cannot come in. My mother legally bought this home, and when she became ill, I moved in to help her. She died, and I inherited this property."

"Yes," said Maciej, "we understand. She just wants to come in and see the home where her father once lived. He, too, died recently."

"No," she said.

"Would you allow her to come into your backyard so she can say a prayer for her grandmother and family who died here?"

"No," the woman repeated. "She can pray where she is standing, since her grandmother owned that lot, too." (So I realized that she knew about my family.)

"Do you know of the Kordash or Jablonski families?" Maciej asked.

"The Kordash family lives around the corner," she said. And with that she left with her dog and abruptly went inside her home.

Maciej left me standing in the back yard of the bus lot, and Bobby continued to film from a distance. As I stood there, I began to imagine my father's life back in the 1920s and '30s. As a young boy, he went to Cheder, a school where boys learned the history, laws, and traditions of the Jewish people, as well as the Hebrew language and prayers. He would have been dressed in black trousers, a white shirt, and black overcoat, with tzitzit (knotted ritual fringes) hanging from the outside of his shirt. A kippah would be covering his head, and payot (lengthy sideburns) would be easily visible on his face.

As he matured into his teenage years, he would have worked alongside his sisters on the family farm, about a mile from here. I imagined the daily hustle and bustle of the Rajrodzki square, across the street from his house, where the townspeople would be buying and selling their wares. Young children would be playing happily nearby, while neighbors would be busy chatting with each other about their families, business, politics, and religion. This small town that was once called Raj, "the city of paradise," turned into sheer hell for its Jews on June 22, 1941. The ground on which I stood had turned into a bloody field. I imagined my father frozen in terror as he watched from his hiding spot next to the house as the uncontrollable mob of his Polish neighbors and the two workers from his farm approached. I tried to visualize his shock as he witnessed his mother being bludgeoned to death and as he watched on with disbelief as his sisters Joshpe and Leah, along with Leah's baby, were savagely murdered—and his being helpless and unable to rescue them. I tried to imagine the horror that penetrated his body as he heard his mother pleading with the murderers to end her life quickly, yet watched as they took their time torturing her. After silence fell, he needed to escape. He fled into the woods, never looked back and never returned home.

All alone in this back yard, I felt compelled to recite the Kaddish out loud. This prayer was for my grandmother, Beila, my Aunt Yoshpe, my Aunt Chaya Esther, my Aunt Leah and her family, and all the martyred souls of Rajgród. I wanted every soul to hear my prayer and to know that they have not been forgotten.

"Yit'gadal v'yit'kadash sh'mei raba," I recited, and immediately my eyes welled up and tears came streaming down my cheeks. "B'al'ma di v'ra khir'utei, v'yam'likh mal'khutei," I slowly continued, and the weeping intensified. "B'chayeikhon uv'yomeikhon," and my voice cracked. Stricken with anguish my tears became uncontrollable. I tried to go on, but I couldn't; my weeping turned into wailing, and all I could do was bawl like a child. These raw emotions consumed me and I could no longer stand erect. I hunched over and buried my head in my palms, continuing to cry for a while. I grieved for all the Jews of Rajgrod and for my father whose world came to an end that day. I mourned the loss of never knowing my grandmother, aunts, uncles and cousins.

Still determined to complete the mourner's prayer out loud, I forced myself to recite each word, which took considerable effort. My laments continued, yet I managed to moan each word, syllable by syllable--O... seh... Sha... lom...--until I had completed the final sentence of the kaddish.

Oseh shalom bimromav, hu ya ase shalom alenu v'al kol yisra'el, v'imru Amen

May the One who causes peace to reign in the high heavens let peace descend on us and on all Israel, and let us say, Amen.

The perception of time had deserted me and after what seemed like a half hour, I began to compose myself. I stood up, wiped the flood of tears from my eyes and face, and concentrated on inhaling deep, slow breaths. These feelings had been intensifying inside of me throughout my journey in Poland. Visiting the ghostly Jewish district of Kazimierz in Cracow was bone-chilling; seeing the infamous death camp of Aushwitz-Birkenau, where over one and a half million Jews were annihilated; and traveling on to Warsaw and Tykotin, where all Jewish life disappeared, was brutally horrifying. These were my people, who had been dehumanized, raped, shackled, tortured, burned, hung, shot, and gassed to death. Then as we had continued to Bialystok, where my great-grandmother, Chana, my great-aunts and -uncles and their families were all murdered, I was overwhelmed on a personal level. And finally reaching Rajgród, standing on the very grounds where my father had witnessed the massacre of his mother and sisters, made it unbearable to restrain my pent-up feelings any further. Venting them was a cathartic moment in my life.

Something fatefully shifted inside of me on that very day. As I stood there I seemed to have struggled internally as if I wrestled with my conscience. I wasn't sure what happened, and didn't understand until I was back home that I faced a choice at that moment: I could either continue my lifelong angst and anguish, feeling bitter, resentful and angry toward the oppressors who had murdered my family and my people; or I could let it all go and forgive them.

My mind fought hard to retain this old way of thinking and being, but deep within me, my soul desperately yearned to change. My soul needed to be liberated. After I unleashed the wails of tears, I felt a sense of relief as if my heritage of suffering was lifted from my entire body; I had let all of the pain go. I didn't want these invasive feelings plaguing my life anymore. They did not spiritually serve me or bring me joy or serenity. I truly desired the peace that reigns with God in the high heavens to descend upon me.

This sense of freedom allows me to remember my people's past without embracing the pain. I will not forget my family. I will not forget the Jews of this tiny shtetl of Rajgród, and I will remember the martyred six million men, women, and children. History will not be erased. Yet I have emerged from Rajgród with a sense of freedom, strength, peace, and finally forgiveness for the enemies of my ancestry.

Though my father was never able to return home, it became my destiny to return for him, for his family, for the Jews of Rajgród, for my people and ultimately for myself.

FOURTEEN

Krystyna Franciska: A Welcome Stranger

Fear makes strangers of people who would be friends.
-Shirley Maclaine

I left the backyard of the bus lot and walked over to Bobby and Maciej, who were waiting for me in front of the house. Both of them were quiet and seemed uneasy around me. They weren't sure what to say, so we walked down the empty dirt roads in silence heading toward the lake to search for the home of Kordash's sister. I was hoping that his sister's children might be able to provide some additional details about the war. Then I wondered about her involvement during this time and whether she might have aided her brother, benefited from his crimes, or possibly helped the Jews. I was also curious if Kordash married and had children after the war—and if they stayed in Rajgród after he was killlled.

I thought about the similarities between Kordash, the Nazis, and all those who were willingly complicit in the murder of the Jews to the nation of the Amalekites of the biblical period. Without any provocation, all these enemies behaved ruthlessly, mercilessly attacking and killing the innocent, unarmed Jewish men, women, and children. In the book of Samuel, God reiterates his commandment to blot out the name of Amalek and to destroy the entire nation by killing every man, woman, infant, ox, sheep, camel, and donkey. This archaic commandment of collective guilt and punishment seemed troubling to me. Are Kordash's family and his descendants guilty by association? Is this current generation of Europeans still to be blamed for their parents' heinous crimes?

Then I thought, am I to be judged on the basis of my father's behavior? I recalled a quote from Elie Wiesel: "Only the guilty are guilty. Their children are not."

As we turned the corner, I began to hear the clucking of chickens, and soon several of them appeared on the road and sidewalk. A short but robust old woman in a dark green babushka hurriedly waddled across the street with her wooden cane. As fast as her feet could take her, she disappeared into the house. This home looked to be well over a hundred years old; there were warped, gray wood panels covering the sides and rooftop of the house, and a muddy path full of puddles led up to the doorway and continued onward towards two run-down barns. Along the sides of the barn were some barrels of hay, a small tractor, a ladder, and some shovels. There were dozens of chickens roaming around the property.

Maciej walked over to the house, knocked on the door, and went inside. Soon both of them came out and we all began to chat. Maciej mentioned that this old woman was afraid of us because there were some men in the neighborhood just a few weeks earlier trying to take advantage of the older people here.

The old woman's name was Krystyna Franciska, and she was born in January 1928 in Rajgród. At a mere 4'10" tall, she was wearing dark pants and a long black skirt covering them; she had a ragged top and a soiled, buttoned-up old knit beige sweater covering most of her body. Her face was aged with deep wrinkles, and her gray hair was visible at the edge of her hairline--underneath the babushka. When she smiled, I noticed that two of her front teeth were missing.

And yet Krystyna appeared very friendly and genuinely eager to answer our questions. Maciej mentioned that I had come from the United States to learn more about the town of Rajgród, where my father was born.

"Did you know of a woman named Beila Szteinsaper?" he asked.

"No," she said.

"She was also known in town as Kachorka," Maciej added.

Krystyna became very quiet and looked downward at the ground in thought. She finally looked up at us and said, "Yes, I remember her. Kachorka was a Jewish lady."

"Can you tell us about her? This woman is her granddaughter," Maciej said as he pointed at me.

Krystyna looked at me and said: "I remember your grandmother. She was a very tall and pretty woman. She lived in the center of town near Maya Street—in the corner house right near the bus station. There was a store right next to her home, and she may have owned it. I would go to the store and buy food. We chatted all the time. She was friendly. Many people in town would go to the store, and we would all talk to one another."

"Bobby," I said in amazement, "can you believe this? She knew my grandmother!"

I stood there in disbelief. How I wished that she spoke English so that I could capture and understand every word she uttered. I was impatient waiting for Maciej to interpret all the details about my family.

"What does Kachorka mean?" I asked.

"It means duckling," Maciej answered.

That makes sense, I thought, because there were quite a few ducks on her farm.

"Do you remember any of Kachorka's children?" asked Maciej. Krystyna thought for a moment and then said "no."

"Do you know if she owned any other property? Maciej asked.

"On the way to Grajewo," Krystyna said, "on the southern outskirts of town she had a farm. The farm was right near the forest, and behind the forest was the lake. It had all been deserted—just a well was left. She was a rich woman. Life was good for all of us before the invasions and before the war."

Krystyna stared at me, looked me up and down and said, "How nice it is for a beautiful American woman to come here to learn about her grandmother."

I smiled and said thank you.

"Did you know the Jablonski or Kordash families?" Maciej asked.

"Kordash's sister came here from Augustow," she said, "which is north of Rajgród, but most of the family has died. There is still the grandson living in the house down the street. They changed their name to Kordashski to sound more Polish."

Then Krystyna looked me over again. "Since you have come to Poland, you will need to learn the language," she said, smiling.

"Tak, tak," I laughed.

"Ask her about when the war started in Rajgród," Bobby suggested. Krystyna remembered all too well when the Russians invaded Rajgród. She spoke in a more somber tone.

"In April 1940, the Russians marched through and occupied this town. They killed my brother, and many of my family members were sent to Siberia. I was left here to work the farm. My husband was also sent to Siberia, but he returned. He has been dead for some time now."

Krystyna continued, "The Russians desecrated the churches. They took down our crosses."

"How did the Russians treat the Jews?" I asked.

"They treated the Jews much better than the Poles," she said.

"Who was left in the town?" I asked.

"There were still people living here. I have been here my whole life."

"When did the Nazis invade?" I asked.

"The Nazis came in 1941 and set up a ghetto near Placa and Maja Streets. A ghetto fence of barbed wire surrounded the area. There were some Polish neighbors trying to hide some Jews, and they were killed. The Jews, the sick, and the old Polish people—along with the gypsies— were taken to the ghetto. Then, eventually, they took everyone from the ghetto and sent them away, but I don't know where they were taken."

"What happened to the synagogues and the mikveh?" I asked.

"The Germans destroyed all of the structures," Krystyna answered.

She pointed toward the lake and said, "Over there is Castle Hill, where there was once a synagogue and a school. The town would gather there on the hill and have special ceremonies. The mikveh was near the lake, and there was another synagogue next to it."

She then looked at me and said, "I can find the gold from within the ashes."

"What does she mean, Maciej?" I asked.

"She has an ability to recognize kind people when she meets them," Maciej said, "and she believes you are a nice person."

Krystyna seemed to be getting tired as she stood leaning on her cane, and yet she invited us all into her home for coffee and tea. She said, "I am getting very old, and I don't know how much longer I have to live."

When we entered her house, we immediately stood in her kitchen. It was a small room, five by seven feet, and we all sat at her table. Her kitchen was untidy: the walls were painted pink, and the wood floors were warped. A worn-out and faded flowered tablecloth covered the table, which had two padded chairs and a couple of wooden stools around it. Yet she was a very gracious host. Her old white double sink was filled with a sweater soaking in water on one side and dirty dishes stacked up on the other side. In the corner of the kitchen she had a coal-burning furnace with large chunks of black coal in a bucket close by. In the other corner was a table with a portable burner set on top to cook food. Below the table were boxes, bags, and some pails protruding from underneath. There was a set of double doors painted yellow leading into her bedroom, and in another corner was a chair where she sat as we drank our coffee. Her tiny bathroom was right near the table; it had a toilet, a bathtub filled to the top with household items, a nonworking washing machine, and a sink.

She made us feel right at home as she brought the cups, coffee, tea, and sugar to the table. We waited for the water to boil and Maciej listened to her talk about her children and grandchildren.

"Did she have any Jewish friends before the war? How did the Jews and Poles relate to one another?" I asked.

"I went to school with the Jewish children," Krystyna said with a smile. "I had a Jewish girlfriend named Bloomka, who was in my class. We would play childhood games together. Bloomka's family would come to buy milk from my farm. We also had a friend named Chaim, who would come to play with us, too. Chaim liked to eat sausage and didn't care that we mixed the milk and meat. I remember his mother's name was Galera and his father's name was Pinchas. I also played at their homes and remember eating matzah. In the wintertime, we would all go sleigh riding down Castle Hill."

Krystyna seemed to enjoy telling us about her earlier childhood memories. "Even though the Jews lived mostly in one area of the town, while the Poles lived in this neighborhood, there was a community and we mostly all got along."

She stood up and went into her bedroom and brought out her papers. She was very proud how neatly she kept her identification papers carefully tucked away. She explained that she gets a pension from the Polish government because her husband was in Siberia.

"I am very lucky," she said. "I am well off and am able to hire a worker to help me manage my farm."

Krystyna was a very warm, charming, and an amiable hostess, and Bobby and I truly enjoyed her company. Before we left, I asked her how many animals she had on the farm. She proudly replied, "I have six dairy cows, seven pigs, and forty chickens on my land."

She led us outside to her barns and showed off her prized possessions. Maciej took a picture of Bobby, Krystyna, and me in front of her barn. We thanked her for her time, left her some money, and told her we needed to move on.

We had barely gotten back on the dirt road when suddenly we heard a dog snarling. Standing at the front of an opened gate to an entrance of a house was a fiendish-looking black dog. He gave us a vicious stare and seemed to say, "Stay away! I will attack if you come close!"

The dog frightened us, and we all walked quickly past the house and continued down the street. I recalled that during my childhood we were never allowed to have a dog; my father would simply not pay to take care of one. But I also noticed that he was quite terrified of them. During the Holocaust, Nazis would use the dogs to intimidate Jews, to hunt them down in the forests, and in some cases to eat them alive. The Nazis were also known to place cancer-causing poison on their teeth. In some concentration camps, dogs were trained to mount naked Jewish women who had been ordered on their hands and knees.

We continued on toward the lake, and I asked Maciej, "Where is the Kordash home? It shouldn't be too far from here."

"We just passed it," he said. "It was the house where that vicious looking dog had growled."

"I guess I was not meant to meet the family. Do you want to go inside the gate and see if anyone is home?" I asked sarcastically.

But Maciej took me seriously, he crossed the road and tentatively walked on the sidewalk and into the front yard. He was nervous, since the dog had disappeared as soon as we had passed by. He called out to see if anyone was at home, but he was too scared to wait, and he quickly retraced his steps.

"I'm sorry, Karen," he said. "I am just too frightened to knock on their door."

We returned to the center of town. We crossed the street near my grandmother's home and walked past a few houses from the corner. It was there that I noticed an indentation on the doorposts of a home. It was evident that this was once a Jewish home and that a mezuzah was once posted on the doorway.[5]

As I stood in front of this home, so close to my grandmother's house, I knew this was the Jewish neighborhood of Rajgród and the site where the Nazis had set up the ghetto. After taking some pictures, we headed back to the van to search for the Jewish cemetery. The sky had darkened, the clouds looked ominous, and the wind had picked up.

Just one mile south of Rajgród, toward Grajewo, off Highway 61 and near the border of another small village (named Opartowa), we found another dirt road leading to another village (named Okoniówce), where we turned off toward the lake. We drove another mile, passed some homes and farms, and ended near a curve in the road where the forest began. There was a ten-foot green pole on the left side of the road, and the forest lay beyond it. We left the van, and the three of us wandered aimlessly into the woods. Maciej had brought along a couple of shovels and some extra gloves, and I carried my umbrella because it had started to rain.

The forest was not quite in full bloom: green leaves had just begun to appear on all the trees and bushes. We brushed away branches in our path as we went deeper into the woods. Maciej saw a small concrete rock and walked toward it. He flipped it over and said that this must be part of a broken mazevah (tombstone). He surveyed the area, grabbed a shovel, and started to bang on the ground. Eventually we heard it hit something hard.

"There is a grave here," he said.

---

5   The mezuzah is a small case, three to six inches long, that is often decorated and contains the first two paragraphs of the Sh'ma. It reminds us of God's presence in our lives and is a declaration of our Jewish identity and faith. Some Jews believe it guards us from the evil spirits.

I saw another small concrete fragment lying 10 feet away, camouflaged by green moss.

"Here's another piece of a mazevah. The graves must be here, too," I shouted.

So I put down my umbrella and began digging and, as I did, I noticed the outline of a grave. Dirt and leaves had been tightly packed over these graves for decades, but I was determined to clear away the debris on this particular gravesite. I dug until I saw thick roots covering the top of a long slab of cement which prevented me from digging any farther. So I used the edge of the shovel and pounded it into the roots, but they didn't completely break. I put down the shovel, straddled my legs over the grave, grasped the roots with my hands and pulled hard. Eventually they snapped and I was able to dig deeper into the earth. The rain poured down, my back ached and my arms were tired but I was determined to uncover this grave. Then I noticed some etchings on the cement.

"Bobby," I yelled, "look here, I found some Hebrew or Yiddish writing on this grave."

"What does it say?" he asked.

"I can't say for sure yet," I said.

So I crouched down on my knees and cleared away the rest of the debris from the top of the gravestone with my hands. "It must be the last name, it looks like the name of Steinblatt."

Then I placed the two fragments of the mazevot (gravestones) near the head of the grave and stood there quietly. In that moment of silence, I thought about my grandfather, Chaim Shlomo, my father's baby brother, Yehuda Leyzer, and all the Jews from Rajgród who were fortunate enough to be buried in a cemetery with something like a dignified funeral. Yet, even in death, they could not escape the evils of anti-Semitism—because the Nazis desecrated these grounds, too. Standing on this forgotten piece of land that was untouched for over seventy years I felt these Jewish souls deserve to rest in peace in a respectable burial place, just like the other cemeteries in Rajgród.

Maciej had a waterproof magic marker, so as we left the forest, I marked the green pole with three Hebrew letters--Shin, Dalet, and Yud--which spells the Hebrew word "Shaddai," God's name. Those letters are an acronym for "Guardians of the Doors of Israel," which sometimes appears on the mezuzah. Then, walking to the edge of the road, where I estimated that the cemetery ended, I found a large tree with a thick trunk at the edge of the road. Grasping the shovel tightly, I carved a Jewish star into the bark. These two markers would make it easier for other descendants of Rajgród to find the cemetery.

As we left the woods, I noticed that my clothes were drenched and my boots, jeans, and gloves were soaked with mud. Physically and emotionally exhausted, I gladly welcomed the three-hour ride back to Warsaw.

It was late at night and the skies were dark when Maciej dropped us off at our new hotel, a location closer to the Old Town Square of Warsaw. As we passed the Warsaw Zoo, Maciej noted: "Recently I guided an Israeli couple from Haifa, and they requested that I take them to this zoo. A few of their relatives survived the Holocaust by hiding underneath the lion's cage."

I was taken aback and thought I heard all the horror stories of the Holocaust and yet there always seemed to be more to uncover. Truly grateful for all his guidance and insight, Bobby and I thanked Maciej and said good-bye. Deep down, I had a strange feeling that this was not going to be the last time I would see him. Tomorrow we would be leaving Poland and flying to Israel. I anticipated the warm and sunny Mediterranean climate and eagerly looked forward to visiting our living relatives and friends in Israel.

When I returned to the United States, I was able to locate additional information about the pogrom and the Nazi invasion of Rajgród. Leb Lewentina, who testified about Rajgród in 1947 at the Jewish Historical Provincial Committee in Bialystok, declared "After the outbreak of World War II, following the stipulations of the Molotov-Ribbentrop Pact, Rajgród came under the Soviet zone of influence. In 1941, after the Nazi invasion of the USSR, the German army overtook the town. A mass execution of about one hundred local Jews was carried out a few days afterwards. In carrying out the extermination, the invaders were helped by Poles, consequently putting Rajgród on the same inglorious list of the towns such as Jedwabne, Wąsosz, or Kolno, where pogroms took place in July 1941.

"In June 1941, as soon as the Germans entered Rajgród, they sent a few Poles such as A-ski,* S-owicz*, and P-ski* to gather one hundred Jews in the marketplace. The above-mentioned Poles went from house to house, and those who refused to go with them were savagely beaten. Among those who were treated this way were Lejb Borowski, a saddler, Szeftel Kacman, [the] Cynowicz family, [the] Rotgeber family, as well as Finklesztejn, a grain trader and the owner of a shop with products exported from outside of Europe. All the Jews were undressed, underwear being the only thing left on their bodies. A 27-year-old daughter of Finklesztejn was given a red flag and all the gathered people, standing four in each row, were supposed to march through the entire town and sing different songs. Their clothes were thrown to the Poles who were catching them. The whole 'ceremony' was directed by two SS men who arrived in the town especially for the purpose of participating in it. At the end, the people were led two kilometers outside the town to the Chojniki forest where they were murdered and buried.

"In the summer of 1941 the Nazis formed a ghetto in Rajgród located around Paca Street. About 1,200 people of Jewish origin, including those displaced from nearby localities, were imprisoned in the ghetto. The ghetto was surrounded with barbed wire. The eldest in the ghetto was 44-year-old illiterate chauffeur, Szyja Grodzie ski, who abused the Jews a lot. The power over the town was in the hands of the town's commandant, who was arrested later in Ełk for cooperation with Germans against the Poles. The Jews did some stone work outside the ghetto. Peasants were also allowed to take the Jews to work, for which they had to pay three marks a day to the German employment agency. The laborers would bring some food to the ghetto. The Poles, when given some money, would bring something to eat too. Rajgród Rabbi Farber was not allowed to leave the ghetto... in 1942, toward evening, all the carts from the town and the surrounding areas were collected, and nobody knew what for. On the next day, all of the Jewish residents from Rajgród were loaded and sent to the ghetto in Grajówo. My mother, Itka Lewintin, and my aunt

Riwa died there. The Jews from Rajgród stayed in Grajewo for six days. Starvation was acute. When a cart was passing, all the Jews would make a dash toward it. From Grajewo they were transported to Bogusze, and from there to Treblinka."

"The cemetery was destroyed during the Second World War. One day the Nazis ordered the deportation of all the tombstones from the Jewish cemetery in Okoniówce. The Jews themselves had to break stones and monuments on the road.....").

The details that I had gathered on the shtetl of Rajgród corresponded to Lejb Lewentin's personal testimonies of the pogrom and ghetto. My father's family was among the first victims of the Rajgród pogrom. Yet, of all my experiences in Rajgród, I obsessed over the fact that I was unable to meet the grandson of Kordash. Why was I was prevented from seeing him? My answers came as I began to think about the people I had actually encountered there.

The woman who refused to let us into her home (my grandmother's house) represents a portion of the Polish population who continue to be fearful for their own survival today. World War II left a devastating impact on the physical and social fabric of Poland, making it the most impoverished country of the war. The Soviets occupied the eastern region of Poland, while the Germans invaded the western region; the Poles were caught between Stalin's communism and Hitler's Nazism. Poland was left in shambles; three major cities—Warsaw, Bialystok, and Lodz—were burnt to the ground, while the remaining three major cities—Cracow, Lwow, and Wilno—suffered other kinds of damage. The countryside of Poland was also laid waste, and the villages, forests, and wildlife were practically destroyed.

After the war Poland was occupied by the Soviet Union, which implemented a regime of terror. Over a quarter of a million Polish soldiers and prisoners of war were murdered, and anyone suspected of revolutionary activity was arrested and sent to work camps. Attempts were made to dissolve religion, the Polish currency, and the culture of the country. Polish schools were burnt down, famine was rampant, and Poland was left isolated from the rest of Europe. Three million Polish men, women, and children also lost their lives during World War II, the second-largest group of people after the Jews. As Poland regained her independence from the Soviet Union in 1989, the Poles who occupied the homes of the Jews were probably fearful that the Jews might return and attempt to confiscate their property. Many Jews have tried to work with international attorneys and the Polish government to be compensated for their land. I am uncertain whether anything has yet materialized.

Krystyna, the old woman, represents a different side of the Polish people. Krystyna graciously welcomed us into her home and treated us respectfully. She appeared to have no prejudices against Jews; indeed, she happily talked about her relationships with her Jewish friends before the war. Some of her family members, like so many other Polish families, were murdered by the Russians and Nazi invaders during World War II. She spoke of the bravery of some of her Polish neighbors who tried to hide Jews, but who paid the ultimate price with their lives. The Polish Resistance, the largest in all of Europe, went underground during the war, fought fervently, and were able to save some Jewish lives. Following World War II, members of the Polish resistance who fought against Hitler were then tortured by the Soviet Union for many decades.

Finally, the dog who stood ferociously at the front gate of the Kordash home represents the evil that still lurks in Poland. Hatred, ignorance, and prejudice still exist there, and it was clear that I was meant to stay away from the descendants of the Kordash family.

FIFTEEN

Israel

If you will it, it is no dream.
-Theodor Herzl

A quarter of a century had passed since my last visit to Israel. I wondered how the country had transformed physically and emotionally over the years. I wondered if Israelis in general were still concerned and affected by the Holocaust and how they were coping with the Palestinian conflict. Though my Hebrew language skills were rusty, I was eager to converse with Israelis. From Ben Gurion Airport, Bobby and I drove to meet a friend who lives in Ashkelon, a Mediterranean coastal town located forty-five minutes south of Tel-Aviv. This once ancient city, occupied by many Biblical nations and foreign empires, is now home to over one hundred thousand Jews. We climbed four long flights of stairs and unloaded our luggage in her apartment, anticipating the magnificent panoramic view of the town and sea. We hugged and barely caught our breath when Shoshana said in a straightforward tone, "When you hear the sirens, run downstairs to the bomb shelter."

Bobby and I stared wide-eyed at each other and I felt my stomach churning. He asked "Where is the bomb shelter?"

"It's on the north side of the building," she answered, "let's go down-stairs and I will show you the entrance." Ashkelon is roughly 13 miles from the Gaza strip, and it had been targeted and attacked by Quassam and Katyusha rockets from the moment Israel forced all Jews out of Gaza in order to return the entire area to the Arab Palestinians. Shoshana mentioned that her daughter's apartment nearby building was bombed a few years back, but everyone survived. It was unsettling knowing that at any time, day or night, an attack could happen. I couldn't imagine having a bomb shelter at the corner of my street in Deerfield, Illinois. I wondered how I would live day-to-day with this lingering threat.

After that gloomy week in Poland, Bobby and I were amazed at the abundance of sunshine. We rented a car and drove north along the border of the West Bank towards the Galilee. We stopped at a McDonalds (but it is Bobby's go-to place when he needs a quick fix), where I saw Jews and Arabs dining together (and I imagined how nice it would be if all it took to bring us together was an occasional Big Mac with fries).

We reached Tiberias, nestled on the Sea of Galilee where the waves were gentle and the sea was gleaming like a sapphire jewel. We traveled onward into the mountains to Safed, an ancient city once home to the great Jewish mystics. The narrow streets were paved with cobblestones and lined with artist galleries. After touring the medieval synagogues, we headed to the border of Israel and Lebanon at Rosh Hanikrah, the cape of the Galilee coast. We walked deep below the chalky, white cliff where the rush of the waters went smashing into the grottos and tunnels. Our day ended with a lovely dinner in Nahariya, a quiet beach town.

Each day of the trip, we had different adventures. We drove through the Judaean Desert and hiked and rested at the Dead Sea, where I lavished my body with the thick, black Dead Sea mud, hoping along with all the other tourists that I could regain my youthful glow. We toured, shopped and dined with family and friends in Old Jaffa and Tel-Aviv and finally, Jerusalem.

In Jerusalem, we visited Yad Vashem, the Holocaust Museum and educational center, hoping to gain more information on Rajgród. The museum was packed with groups of young IDF soldiers in uniform, many carrying their weapons. These young Israeli men and women are required to participate in a day seminar. "Why is this a requirement?" I asked one of the soldiers.

"Just a generation ago we faced extinction. We had no Jewish army to protect us, and the world didn't come to our aid when 6 million Jews were killed. Now we do have a Jewish army, and that army must understand how Israel became a Jewish state."

We left the museum without having gained any new information about Rajgród. A few days later as we were driving back to Ashkelon, we heard the Memorial Day siren that is blasted each year in memory of fallen Israeli soldiers. We stopped our car and stood outside in silence, as did all Israelis, until the siren ended. We were told that every single Israeli has either lost someone or knows of someone who died in battle or from a terrorist attack. That evening Shoshana took us to the city square for the start of Memorial Day ceremonies that lasted through the following day. We sat with hundreds of Israelis listening to a bereaved father tearfully speak about his son who had recently been killed. We watched children reciting and performing reflective songs while two large screens showed a continuous list of names and pictures of fallen soldiers. The ceremony ended with a rabbi reciting the mourners' prayer.

A veil of sadness loomed over the crowd and the next generation of Israelis continue to mourn; when will this ever end? At that moment, I received a text message from my eldest son, Max. "Happy Mother's Day! Love you! And thank some Israeli soldier from me, too." I was chilled by Max's timing and had to wipe away some tears with my sleeve.

Profoundly moved by this Memorial Day observance, my mind reverted back to Rajgród. There were no monuments in the town square or at the cemetery to remember the Jews of Rajgród. No one would have ever known that a thriving Jewish community existed there. I wondered if it would be possible to restore the cemetery and erect a memorial to commemorate the martyred souls of Rajgród.

"Don't waste your money on building one," commented my rabbi after we'd returned home, "put it into Hebrew Day School education."

After hearing my idea, Bobby said, "The Poles aren't ready for a monument in their town. It would be vandalized like other Jewish sites in Poland."

Because restaurants and theaters are generally closed on this day (in contrast to Memorial Day in United States), we, like most of the country, attended a ceremony and watched T.V. programs in which fallen soldiers were honored or Israel's wars were discussed. As the sun was setting, Shoshana led us back to the square where we'd watched the ceremony the previous evening. But the mood had shifted, and people wore festive clothing as excitement buzzed through the crowd.

Shoshana explained that Memorial Day sadness gave way to Independence Day joy. "We are filled with pride and dignity. Finally, we have a homeland. As sad as we felt all day, we understand that our soldiers sacrificed their lives so that we could build a future for our children."

We watched fireworks light the skies over Ashkelon. Then Shoshana drove us to a party in a nearby moshav (settlement town). White lights flickered in the trees surrounding the party area and dozens of tables were decorated with flowers and flags. Bobby nudged me towards a table covered with delicious looking baba ganoush, hummus, and tabouleh where we loaded our plates, leaving room for perfectly grilled kabobs. I sipped fruity, full-bodied wine and loosened up enough to sing along to the old Israeli folk songs being broadcast from large speakers. The women jumped out of their seats as the music sped up, and we danced in circles for over an hour while Bobby sipped on his scotch.

I was a little surprised when most of the men (including Bobby) joined all of us women in dancing to a Michael Jackson song. I thought it was funny to mark the beginning of Israel Independence Day with American pop music.

The next day Shoshana, Bobby and I met a tour guide in the old city of Jerusalem. With a bit of apprehension, we walked through the empty four quarters of this ancient city. Many of the shops and restaurants were closed and the streets were lined with Israeli police and soldiers. While the Israelis are celebrating their Independence, the Palestinians are observing Nakba Day, "The Day of Catastrophe." This is their annual day to commemorate their displacement as a result of the 1948 war. On this day, many tourists avoid the Old City for fear of a terrorist attack. All day long, Shoshana kept calling home to check on her family and our tour guide was listening to the radio for any possible incidents. In the City of David, a Jerusalem neighborhood, an Israeli woman was assaulted by Arab stone throwers since she had an Israeli flag flying from her car as was captured on local security cameras.

An Israeli Arab plowed into a crowded street in Tel-Aviv injuring many and killing one Israeli. Arab infiltrators crossed the Israel-Syria cease fire line and 14 of them were killed by the Israeli army.

We purchased tickets to tour the underground, excavated tunnels at the foot of the Temple mount near the Western Wall. For centuries this area has been of utmost religious importance, in particular to the Jews and Moslems. In 1996 Benjamin Netanyahu permitted the Jews to open the northern end of this tunnel wall and controversy arose which resulted in riots and more killings between the Israelis and Palestinians. We walked underneath Jerusalem into a subterranean Roman city through vaulted medieval chambers and tunnels. These forgotten ruins from two-thousand years ago were endlessly fascinating. I was astonished to hear from our tour guide that prior to the Roman siege of Jerusalem and the destruction of the Holy Temple, the Jewish zealots killed over ten thousand Jews in Jerusalem. Many of the Jerusalem Jews wanted to negotiate with the Romans while the zealots wanted to fight to the bitter end.

The following night, Bobby and I met Avi at charming Cafe Suzanna in a trendy neighborhood of Tel-Aviv called Neve Tzedek. We sat outside on the cafe's terrace and spent hours talking about Rajgród, our parents and politics.

"Your father accused my mother of taking the salami from him as a child," Avi said with a smile, "all these years later and he was still very upset."

"He never forgave her," I replied with a smirk.

"My mother's version of the story was different. She told me that she thought the food and the salami was for her. She shared it all with her friends. She didn't think she did anything wrong," he said and we all laughed.

"After visiting Rajgród, Karen, can you believe that our parents were afraid of the Poles?"

"Avi," I responded, "it was a different era and a different generation of Jews. The Jewish mentality back then tolerated behaviors that are unacceptable today. It certainly does not depict the mentality of today's tough Israeli Jew."

Avi agreed.

"Why do you think your parents did not express any interest in your trip to Poland? Did they ever want to talk about their past? Why were you so interested in going to Poland?" I asked.

Avi answered, "I strongly believe in connecting to my roots, that is why I went back to Poland. When the country of Israel was established they wanted to disconnect and disassociate from the cultural background of the Eastern European Jews. My parent's generation desired a new Jewish character. Personally, I believe this disconnection was an excuse. They had a difficulty dealing with the Holocaust and preferred to block the emotional charge related to the fact that they left their parents and escaped. They carried a lot of guilt, but no one can judge."

Avi relayed a story about how his parents met before the war. "My mother, Tova, was best friends with a girl who was dating my father, Chaim. All three were planning to go to Palestine in 1939 with a group of other Jewish pioneers, but this girl needed to remain in Poland to take care of her ailing mother. Tova and Chaim left for Palestine without her and she died during the Holocaust with her family. My parents carried plenty of guilt that lasted their lifetime. Guilt for leaving their friend, guilt for leaving their families behind, guilt for marrying each other, and guilt for surviving," he said. Living with survivor's guilt was quite debilitating to them and left scars on Avi and his older brother, Tali. The next generation was clearly impacted by the Holocaust.

"Karen, your trip to Poland has inspired me to return there. I want to have the cemetery of Rajgród cleaned up. It should not be that costly. I will look into the details."

"Avi," I said, "I also want to build a monument in memory of all the victims who perished in Rajgród during World War II." I thought about how my father never achieved his goal to erect a monument in the city of Chicago in memory of the six million Jews. I felt destined to make this happen in Rajgród.

By 11 p.m. we left the restaurant and Avi drove us to the Azrieli Center, a trio of contemporary skyscrapers. While we sipped our cappuccinos on the top floor of the circular tower and pierced at the twinkling skyline, Avi shared historical details of Tel-Aviv. It was long after midnight, we drove back to Neve Tzedek and said our goodbyes. I was certain that Avi would follow through with our plan to restore the cemetery of Rajgród.

As we packed up our bags for our return flight to Chicago, I thought about how unsettling it is for the Israelis to live day-to-day in fear and wondered the same about the Palestinians. Can peace ever be achieved between them in my lifetime? Can they learn to let go of their past and forgive each other? But how can they forgive each other if they are presently living the conflict?

SIXTEEN

Where Do We Go From Here?

Hatred does not cease by hatred. Only by love.
–Gautama the Buddha

W orld War II ended in 1945, but the war continued to rage within my father. He had a right to be angry. Everything that he loved was destroyed. Most Jews in Europe succumbed to death during the Holocaust, but he survived. Had he been sensitive or delicate in the face of his experiences, he might very well have collapsed and died. By grasping and holding onto his anger, he created a very hard and tough exterior that helped him remain strong and vigilant.

But his anger was out of control, and it turned him into a raging inferno. He became violent and easily agitated—and he learned to hate. The extreme hostility that his enemies spewed on him, he learned to spew on everyone around him. His struggle for survival fueled his hatred: he became like someone on a killing rampage, where nothing can stop the rage. It ravished his system and poisoned his insides. He was tormented and killed any love that he might have had within himself and his family.

Hatred turned Jacob and Esau against each other for twenty years. Hatred turned Joseph's brothers against him and shattered their families' lives. Hatred is so strong that it divides families, divides people within communities, and divides countries. It spreads like a wildfire to those around us and burns the ones we love. Hatred perpetuates hatred.

Sadly, the Tutsi survivor spoke of the massacre and said, "The neighbors of our village started killing my family. They took my parents and tied their hands and feet and took them to the river. Some jumped right in to escape the machine-gun fire, while some needed to be pushed into the river bed. After stealing our livestock and everything from our homes, they set our houses on fire."

Another victim said: "My family and I escaped from our home and ran to my uncle's house. We stood outside in his front yard begging him to help us, but he refused. He told the officials to take us, the 'vermin,' away. He said he did not know who we were. I survived the genocide, but my whole family was murdered."

Another woman recalled, "Our parents were good friends and they got along together. Before the massacre, we worked and lived peacefully in the same neighborhood. I was incapable of telling the ethnic groups apart. I didn't even know that I was a Tutsi. My mother, brothers, and sisters were all killed. I was left as a pregnant widow with my six children. A Hutu neighbor hid us from the massacre. I was forced to give birth in a bush, hiding with my children while listening to the chilling screams of my family and others being murdered in the village." [6]

When President Habyarimana of Rwanda, a Hutu, was assassinated, the violence in Rwanda spiraled out of control, creating some of the bloodiest events of the twentieth century. In this small east African country, the Hutu government openly organized and meticulously targeted a genocide against the Tutsis of Rwanda. From April to July 1994, the death toll rose to almost one million people. Ethnic cleansing first began with the use of identification cards to separate the Tutsis from the Hutus. Skin color was also a factor of separation, since the Tutsis appeared lighter. The Tutsis were kept apart from the general population and became the Hutus' slaves and targets of rape. Even though they both shared the same religion—many on both sides were Catholic—that did not stop the killings.

When this premeditated genocide ended, the country of Rwanda struggled to find justice for its citizens. The survivors returned to

---

6 Rwanda: Living Forgiveness Videotape.

their villages to rebuild their homes and farms. With over 120,000 perpetrators incarcerated, a new system of justice, called Gacaca, was implemented by the new Rwandan government. Gacaca promotes unity and reconciliation by bringing together the perpetrators and the survivors. The perpetrators are encouraged to publicly confess their crimes face to face with the survivors, and to ask to be forgiven by the surviving members of the families they murdered. Survivors receive counseling, and many are able to forgive their enemies. The perpetrators then return to the villages of the survivors and help them rebuild their demolished homes. They are able to work, to live, and to pray once again--together within their community. These Rwandans have demonstrated the powerful effects of forgiveness. They continue to teach us that a nation can learn to heal and overcome centuries of a painful and turbulent history and return to a place of reconciliation among its people.

Looking back at the year I studied with Sister Maria at the Claret Center, I now can fully appreciate and understand her profound disposition. She was filled with a sense of tranquility as she continued to seek out spiritual training to comfort and aid herself and her people in Rwanda. Any traces of trepidation, resentment or despair that resonated within her had disappeared. When she forgave those who murdered her family, her wounds began to heal. She was no longer a victim, no longer a child or a sister of a survivor—but a spiritual leader and healer.

In the Spring of 2011, I met a woman named Liz, who openly shared stories of her tumultuous childhood with me. "My father's fears, confusion, and angst from his experiences during World War II affected his entire life. One moment he was gentle, telling me a funny story; the next moment he was full of rage," said Liz.

Liz's father had acute migraine headaches, just as my father did, and was explosive and physically and emotionally abusive toward his family.

"If my father lost control," she said, "I would run. Anyone in our family would be at risk of being killed. He beat up my one of my brothers so badly that a few times I thought he had killed him. I never had a friend—not once—spend the night at my home. When I became a teenager, I turned to alcohol. I had taken all the pain of my childhood inside me and held on to my victimization."

I mentioned to Liz that her father reminded me of mine, yet there was one distinct difference between them. Her father, a German, was drafted as a teenager into the Hitler Youth Movement, where he had learned to kill Jews. Liz's adult life was stricken with depression, alcohol addiction and unhealthy relationships. She said that her healing began when she forgave her father.

When our bodies are subjected to physical wounds, the pain usually dissipates as the body naturally restores itself. Often a scar is visible as a reminder of the experience. However, if we prod and pick at the wound, it remains open to contamination, healing is prevented, and the pain ensues. My father was never able to heal from his wounds and never achieved a serene life. He was never going to forgive his enemies: until his death he remained the wounded survivor, the wounded partisan, the wounded husband, the wounded father, the wounded grandfather, the wounded Jew—and ultimately the wounded child of God.

Life provides us with people who challenge us. God brought my father into my life to teach me one of the most valuable lessons: the lesson of forgiveness. My father, Arie Kaplan, became the greatest teacher in my life, and for that I am indebted to him. The hatred that once resonated within me toward him has vanished. There are no regrets from my childhood experiences. Each experience has given me the opportunity to learn and grow in life. Resonating within me is a compassionate, forgiving, and loving heart toward my father. Forgiving him has allowed me to heal and move forward.

Throughout the afflicted history of Jews, the Holocaust remains the ultimate catastrophic event. Our indignation toward Hitler and the perpetrators of the Holocaust continue to enslave us and we perpetuate these thoughts and feelings onto our children; we have not been able to move forward from that tragic period of our history. Can we learn to deal with the pain, emotionally process it, and let it go? Is it possible to teach our children to be free and to love again? Can we forgive Hitler and all the oppresors of the Holocaust? Can we begin to heal?

We cannot bring peace to this planet if we are filled with anger and hatred. I want to create a world of forgiveness, not a world of judgment. And I want to instill these values in my children. I want my children and grandchildren to understand that forgiveness brings you to an internal place of peace and creates a loving world around you. Peace begets peace. "Hatred does not cease by hatred, only by love." Every soul is a child of God. Every soul is derived from the same source, and has a right to be healed. Regardless of what a soul has done in life, every soul has a right to return to God. Hitler, too, had a soul: like me, he was a child of God.

Returning to my father's home in Poland and standing on my family's land was a poignant and life-changing moment. Resonating within me were the bitterness, sadness, and hatred that I had stored from my ancestry. In this remote shtetl of Rajgród, I had penetrated to a deep place within me where the pain and suffering of my family and ancestors had engulfed my being. I had a choice to cleave to those lifelong debilitating feelings or allow them to surface and purge them. My soul was finally free as I bellowed out of the pangs of my painful lineage. Relief came to my body, and I finally began to feel at peace.

I chose to forgive Pharaoh and the Egyptians for our enslavement in Egypt. I chose to forgive the Amalekites in the desert of Sinai. I chose to forgive the Babylonians and the Romans for destroying our Holy Temple and uprooting us from our homeland. I chose to forgive King Ahasuerus and Haman. I chose to forgive the Crusaders, the English, the Germans, the Prussions, the Russians, the French, the Spaniards, the Venetians, the Cossacks, the Poles and the Nazis. I chose to forgive Hitler. I also chose to forgive my own people, the Jewish extremists who murdered our own during the Roman invasion and the Maccabean revolt.

Remember, God doesn't give us the people we want; God gives us the people we need—to help us, to hurt us, to leave us, to love us, and to make us into the people we were meant to be.

To my dear father, Arie, I have forgiven you, and now for the first time I can say I love you. Free at last, I have finally come home.

Karen Kaplan and her children, from left,
Noah Boton, Raquel Boton and Max Boton.

EPILOGUE

Life will give you whatever experience is most helpful for the evolution of your consciousness.
-Eckhart Tolle

It had been months since my children were all home and I couldn't wait to be with them. Max had started his first job teaching high school history and coaching basketball. He stayed at his dad's house during the week (since it was closer to his work), and came home on weekends. Noah and Raquel were both in school at the University of Illinois-Champaign Urbana and I hadn't seen them since the new year. They came in for spring vacation, and Raquel had been sleeping in my room the past four nights.

"Mom, I decided to stay in my room tonight."

"What ever you want, Sweetheart," I said, "it's late and I'm going to bed."

She tucked me in, kissed me on my forehead and said "good night mom, love you and sweet dreams."

Raquel went into her room and I fell asleep watching T.V. Noah was downstairs at the kitchen table with earphones on, listening to a lecture on his computer as he studied for his MCAT exams.

Minutes before 11:00 p.m. three armed, masked men stormed into our house through the open garage door. They headed directly to the kitchen, grabbed Noah, and threw him on the floor, facedown. They tied his hands behind his back and bound his feet together. One of the gunmen took Noah's cell phone and zapped it in the microwave. Then he slammed Noah's computer to shut off the din.

"How many are upstairs and where are they?" one of them demanded.

"Two, I don't know where they are," cried Noah.

While one gunman guarded Noah, the other two ran upstairs. I awoke to two gunmen who stood at the front of my bed and pointed their weapons at me. One of them was dressed in blue medical scrubs and a surgeon's mask. The other wore sunglasses and a dark hat that covered his forehead and ears.

"Who are you? Who are you?" I screamed and thought for a split second this must be a prank. I jumped out of bed and instinctively tightened the long cotton robe around my body, wishing I'd also worn a nightgown. The gunman who wore the scrubs pulled down his mask and yelled, "Give me your hands." He grabbed my arms and tied them together with large garbage bag ties.

"Where's the cash? Where's the cash?" he screamed in a viscous tone. I was so scared I felt like I wasn't even in my body.

I cried out, "I don't have any cash. Take me to the bank. I'll give you all my money." I remember thinking that I wanted them to take me out of the house so that they wouldn't harm my children. But he slammed me into the night stand and pushed me down onto the floor. He stood over me pointing the gun at my head. He seemed to be waiting while I just stared at the gun.

Then the third gunmen looked in my bathroom and ran down the hallway. What I didn't know was that Raquel had heard my screams. She'd locked her bedroom door and hid in the corner of her room. The gunman kicked her door open and barged into her room. He saw her crouched behind the dresser with a cell phone to her ear.

He put the gun barrel to her temple and yelled, "Give me the phone!"

She gave him the phone, pointed to her bed and cried, "there's my wallet and tablet. Take it."

He hurried out of her room, calling out to the thug who was still holding me at gunpoint, "Hey dude, she called 911."

As they bolted downstairs, I sprang up and left my room to watch them. I hoped they had all left the house. I ran back to the bedroom and managed to dial help with my arms still tied. Then I went to find Raquel. She stood in her doorway looking shocked and pale, but didn't appear to be physically injured.

A woman answered my call and I screamed "men just broke into my home. They had guns. Come quickly!" Raquel and I dashed downstairs and found Noah still bound on the kitchen floor. She ran to the cabinets and found a pair scissors to cut him free.

I darted to the front door and saw it was locked. I raced to the door leading to the garage and locked it. Emergency services were still on the phone. "Where is the police?" I wailed.

"They are there" she answered, "stay on the phone".

"I don't see them. Where are they?" I screamed.

"They have surrounded your house."

Each second on the phone felt like hours. I couldn't stop shaking. My children and I huddled in the foyer together. She spoke up again. "There is an officer walking up your driveway. Do you see him?"

"Yes" I answered .

"Let him in," she said and I hung up.

The officer told us to come outside and led us to our next door neighbor's house. It was 30 degrees outside and we were shivering, shaking, and I felt sick. My neighbor let us in and gave us blankets and socks. She found a pair of scissors and cut me free. My arms were noticeably scraped and bruised from the rough edges of the zip ties.

The police taped the perimeter of my house. They spent the next couple of hours searching for clues and fingerprinting every door and handle. We were eventually driven to the police station. They took us downstairs to a small room and we all sat on a couch. Noah had his arms around me and Raquel sat closely at my side.

Tears began streaming down my cheeks. I turned to Noah and sobbed, "My poor baby...I can't imagine what went through your mind when the gunmen raced upstairs."

I cried for my children having to endure this unfathomable experience; did they think we were all going to die?

"This is a bizarre crime," said the detective, "do any of you have an idea about who might want to hurt you? Do any of you have enemies?"

I didn't know what to think, but couldn't imagine anyone who could be so vicious that they would hire gunmen to harm us. They questioned us together and then separately for a couple of hours wanting to know both every detail of the home invasion and information about our personal lives.

"You are all very lucky," said the officer. "This could have been a whole lot worse.

This crime is considered one notch below a murder. Thankfully your daughter had the quick wits to dial 911."

Bobby came to police station just minutes after I called him. The officers brought us upstairs to meet him. He tightly wrapped his arms around me and said, "Are you all ok? I can't believe this has happened."

The police officer suggested Bobby return home; the investigation was not complete.

"Can we all sleep in your house tonight?" I asked Bobby.

"Of course, I'll get everything ready for your family," he said and left.

We finished answering all the detective's questions and they drove us back home. The smell of burnt metal and plastic was noticeable as soon as we entered our house. Max was there waiting for us and hugged each one of us.

"Look around and see if they took anything," said the detectives.

After a few minutes of searching I said, "Just my purse."

"Tomorrow you need to come back to the station for facial composites. Also, in the next few days, all of you, including Max, need to be fingerprinted," said the detectives.

By 3:30 a.m. my children and I drove to Bobby's house and spent the rest of the night there. Raquel and I shared a bedroom once again while my sons slept in another room. I didn't sleep that first night (or for many weeks afterward).

In the morning a security company came to change my locks and the following day a wireless alarm system was installed.

"Raquel," I said, "the alarm technician gave me this panic button free of charge since he felt so sorry me. It can be worn around my neck when I'm at home. I press and hold this button for 2 seconds and the police will come immediately."

"Mom," said Raquel, "don't wear your fear."

"You're right, but it will take some time to heal." I said.

"Fine, I'll give you one week." she said and I smiled for the first time since the home invasion.

Why would armed thugs want to invade my home? There is no money stashed here and I don't work in a cash business or handle any cash transactions. Was it random? Maybe it was opportunistic? After all, the garage door was accidentally open. But I notice lots of homes in my neighborhood where the garages are left open and many of my friends leave their doors unlocked. A crime like this has never occurred in Deerfield. Could I have been the intended target? Did someone follow any of us home that day? These questions kept replaying over and over in my mind - day after day.

Staying home alone during the day or night was not an option. I was terrified. When Noah and Raquel went back to school, friends came by to keep me company. Bobby's golden retriever, Lucky, stayed with me during the day until I finally adjusted to being home by myself. My panic button was my safety guard yet it felt like an albatross around my neck. It was a constant reminder of the home invasion.

Bobby and I took turns sleeping at each other's places. While he slept, I would lay awake listening to the noises inside and outdoors. Muffled sounds agitated me. I followed the movement of lights on the bedroom ceiling and walls as the cars drove by. If the lights slowed down or stopped, I ran to the side of the window and looked to see if a car had parked on the street. I was paranoid. If Bobby woke up to go to the bathroom at night, and I awoke seeing his silhouette, I screamed. My startling reflex intensified. I was scared of my own shadow.

My children returned from college in May and new rules were implemented in our house. If they came home after 10 p.m., they would call or text before they entered the house. What if someone was waiting in the bushes ready to hurt them? From my upstairs window, I watched as they walked up the driveway into the house.

Being in my car felt safer but I always checked my rear view mirrors to see if I was being followed. I would be on the look out of strange cars parked in my neighborhood. My friends and family members suggested that I move. My house did not feel like a home so I put it up for sale. It sold within two weeks and I bought a condo in an adjacent suburb. A new beginning and a safer environment is just what I needed.

Even with the prospect of moving, my nerves were getting the best of me. I couldn't help but think about the very day my father witnessed his mother and sisters taken from their home and beaten to death. Though my experience was an inkling of what my father endured, I was in a hyper-vigilant state of fear, just like him. Was I following in his footsteps destined to be paranoid and fearful for the rest of my life? Was I continuing centuries long heritage of fear and victimization? Was it ever going to be possible to let this go and move forward with grace and ease?

A couple of months passed and I was feeling less vulnerable and more secure in my house. During this time, I met with a social worker who thought I was doing quite well under the circumstances. But I noticed that my fear was morphing into anger. I wanted those bastards caught and visualized them rotting in jail. How dare they threaten my family. How dare they scar my children for life. I wanted justice and I wanted it now. Each week I contacted the sergeant and detectives at the Deerfield police station hoping for new information on my case. The fingerprints came back negative with just traces of my daughter's prints on her cell phone. Each day I checked the internet for the latest articles involving current arrests of home invaders in the Chicago metropolitan area. I looked at countless mugshots online, but my case was still a mystery. These thugs are roaming the streets, I thought and terrorizing other families. They must be stopped and held accountable for their crimes.

Again I thought about my father focusing his entire life on revenge and plotting the deaths of Kordash and Jablonski, (the workers who murdered my grandmother and aunts). He never discovered that they were killed after the war. Maybe the criminals that invaded my home are already serving a jail sentence. I may never know.

What I do know is that I am tired of feeling scared, anxious and paranoid. I am tired of feeling bitter and angry. This fear and anger will consume me if I let it persist. I don't want to be just a survivor or a victim.

I want to be able to go outside at night and return home without fear. I want to live my life with fortitude, hope and optimism.

Amidst all these feelings, a bewildering question echoed in my mind. Why did this incomprehensible experience happen to me? Maybe it was a divine plot designed to test whether I can recover from a traumatic episode. Maybe this was my ultimate test of forgiveness...to forgive those who might have raped and murdered my children and me.

I cried knowing that my children were deeply traumatized and yet part of me was grateful that they were home that evening. If not for them, I may not be alive today. I was seconds away from rape, torture and possibly death. Then I wondered why Noah and Raquel needed to experience this trauma, as well.

I hope these three hoodlums will be caught and sent to jail. They're probably going to try other home invasions, and they'll most likely be incarcerated one day. But I don't want to worry about if and when they will be punished because it just isn't up to me. I don't want to be consumed by what is going to happen to them. But I know that my hatred of these men is like a set of crab claws hooked inside of me. It can sometimes smother my thoughts, control my feelings, and waste my time and energy. What I can do is not let this experience destroy my equilibrium. I cannot control the wheels of justice, but I can learn to control my emotions and not let them get the best of me.

People who have bumped up against evil are often consumed by what should happen to the evil-doers. Sometimes they even get bogged down fantasizing about revenge in addition to demanding justice. My father, for example, spent his whole life in a place of darkness and never even considered the idea of moving on. He was paralyzed by his feelings and his quest for compensation. Letting go of rage and forgiving those who had harmed him wouldn't have changed anything except for his outlook on life and its domino effect on the next generation.

After twenty-one years raising my three children in my Deerfield home, I eagerly packed up the entire house and counted the days until I moved. Will I be able to create a new home for my family filled with laughter and joy? Can I rise above this trauma and allow myself to feel peace in my heart? I want everyone who has suffered to be able to overcome it, and to return to a place of wholeness.

Looking to the external is not going to help any of us; the answer lies deep in our cores. Others have said this in different ways, but the truth is that we can't usually affect the world just by holding onto anger and fear. Nothing is going to change, because the only possible change is inside of us.

Lying in bed feeling hurt, persecuted, fearful or otherwise mistreated is not going to lead to a better way of life for anyone. Nor is it going to solve anything. I don't want to lose anymore precious time consumed with these feelings. Just like everyone else in my position, I needed to return to the peace and contentment that once resided within me, to channel my fear into positive thoughts, and to remain calm and centered.

I know that even when bad things happen, I will have the strength and control to overcome the kind of pessimism and defeatism that plagued my father throughout his life. Of course I understand that I need to be careful and cautious, but I refuse to let my self be alarmed or paranoid any longer. As the months passed, my thoughts about the home-invasion became less frequent. But whenever I start to see images of those invaders and the tension begins to mount, I distract myself. I take long deep breaths and remind myself that I love life with every cell and fiber of my being. I remind myself that I am created in the image of a loving God. I visualize a feminine presence for God (called the Shechinah in Hebrew), which I feel as a protective covering or shield surrounding me. I repeatedly chant the words of the Adon Olam:

"I entrust my soul in God's hands, when I sleep and when I awake, and with my spirit and my body. God is with me, I will not fear."

And if none of these steps works for me in overcoming the tendency to dwell on my anger and fear, I take the next step. I picture very large hands of God, and imagine those men enveloped in those hands. Let God take care of them, I pray. Then I say the following:

I want to honor myself,

I want to honor the memory of my father,

I want to honor my ancestors.

I want to give hope to the next generation.

I forgive those home invaders.

APPENDIX

———

Here is a current list of just a few programs of Holocaust education in my community and worldwide.

1. Area congregations and schools continue to provide lectures on the Holocaust and anti-Semitism. Recently, my synagogue office displayed a book called "Holocaust Survivor COOKBOOK" as a fundraiser for the preschool.

2. The "Holocaust Cantata" is a recent program sponsored by two synagogues and a church performing music written by the inmates of the Nazi concentration camps.

3. The "World Federation of Jewish Child Survivors of the Holocaust" unites children who survived the Holocaust and hosts conferences worldwide.

4. "March of the Living" is an international program geared mostly for Jewish teenagers to march on the soil of Auschwitz to Birkenau, the largest concentration camp complex in Poland, where over one million Jews were gassed and cremated. Some of my friends have sent their children on this program or similar ones where teenagers spend a week in Poland learning about the Holocaust.

5. In 2009, the Illinois Holocaust Museum and Education Center in Skokie, Illinois, opened. Dedicated to preserving the memories of the victims perished in the Holocaust, it strives to educate the world communities to confront racism, hatred and genocide that exist in our world today. This particular program is valuable because it strives to educate all communities of the Midwest. My

friends and several of their parents have committed to volunteer and train as docents leading group tours throughout the museum. Some of their college age children have applied for internships to gain insight and experience working at the museum.

Bar and Bat Mitzvah-age children can participate in twinning with a child who perished in the Holocaust. By exploring and learning about the life of a persecuted child prior and during World War II, the Bar and Bat Mitzvah children create a personal connection to the suffering of the children.

6. The Holocaust Educational Foundation and Northwestern University have an intensive two-week program for prospective Holocaust educators.

7. The Anti-Defamation League of Chicago provides Holocaust education workshops for over 6,000 community leaders and educators.

8. The United States Holocaust Memorial Museum opened in 1993 in Washington D.C. and situated among our national monuments. The museum contains Steven Spielberg's film and video archives. Spielberg's Shoah Foundation has recorded over fifty thousand video testimonies of the many survivors of the Holocaust including Jehovah's Witnesses, homosexuals and gypsies. Also included are political prisoners, survivors of Hitler's eugenics policies, liberators and war crime trial participants spanning over fifty-six countries and thirty-two languages.

9. The U.S. Holocaust Museum has helped launch monthly meetings for children of survivors to share their backgrounds and explore topics related to the Holocaust.

10. "Names Not Numbers" is an intergenerational program to help the younger generation learn firsthand about the Holocaust. The teens interview and videotape Holocaust survivors and create a film based on the testimonies. My alma mater elementary school, Hillel Torah in Skokie, is one of the many schools throughout the country involved with this project.

A Note From The Author

All the years of suffering from my disconsolate relationship with my father have faded into distant memories. The rewards of forgiving my father has allowed me to gain a higher perspective of him and emotionally soften inside. As a result, I want to help my children understand the powerful effects of forgiveness. I want to make a difference in my life and help bring about peace.

These past few years, I have volunteered and served as a board member for an organization called Hands of Peace (HOP). HOP is an interfaith, two week summer program for Israeli, Palestinian and American teenagers held in the northern suburbs of Chicago. Together they attend intense dialogue sessions, learn peace building and leadership skills and develop personal relationships with each other.

One summer during HOP, I hosted an Israeli girl from a settlement town who had never met a Palestinian. She seemed irritated by a particular Arab girl in her dialogue session who consistently appeared resentful and angry. As the final days of the program approached, many teens felt sad about leaving and were crying. Yet this Arab girl appeared unbothered. On the last day of HOP, this Israeli girl walked into the bathroom and found the Arab girl huddled alone in the corner crying. The Israeli girl told me that she had done something unthinkable. She walked over to the Arab girl and wrapped her arms around her. Together they both cried.

That evening, upon receiving the HOP "Olive Branch" award at the final banquet ceremony, I delivered this speech.

"Bekash Shalom VeRodfehu"

This Hebrew expression literally means one should desire peace and chase after it. To dream of peace is not sufficient; one must be proactive and pursue it. How can we pursue peace? The Hebrew word Shalom (peace) is derived from the root word Shalem - meaning complete. It is essential that we first feel content, whole and tranquil within ourselves so that we can go into the world and help others.

That is a tough challenge. Many of you come from hostile and traumatic backgrounds which would make it difficult to find the inner calm. By clinging to life's bitter experiences we continue our suffering. We become paralyzed with resentment, anger and fear.

I personally understand the difficulty of letting go of a tragic past. My father was a Holocaust survivor, witnessed the death of his mother and two sisters and was forcibly expelled from his home in Poland. He survived several years in the brutal forests of Eastern Europe while the rest of his family was sent off to the gas chambers at Treblinka. He carried his pain and anger close to his heart. He was unable to let go of his past. My childhood was filled with chaos and violence. I, too, suffered.

We all have difficult choices to make in our lives. I chose to forgive my father. I also chose to forgive all the oppressors of the Holocaust who had murdered my family and six million of my people. I feel liberated and at peace, today, because of my decision.

I challenge each one you to open up your hearts to forgiveness, open up your hearts to love, and let go of the pain. Stop this endless cycle of hatred and retaliation. Cast away your anger, put down your weapons. All of you deserve to live in peace.

Bekash Shalom Verodfehu - may you find serenity in your hearts, so that you can go forward into the world and obtain peace.

Another peace initiative in my area is sponsored by the Rotary of Highland Park. Their focus is fostering peaceful coexistence between

Catholic and Protestant teenagers from Northern Ireland. After spending time with these teens, I discovered their ardent desire to resolve their differences and create a harmonious future together. Their willingness to let go of their past gives me hope. We visited the Illinois Holocaust Museum and learned about the tragic effects of prejudice during the Holocaust and discussed the existence of hatred today in America, Ireland and throughout the world.

Lastly, my personal mission of building and erecting a monument for the Jewish cemetery of Rajgród has progressed into the final stages. Together with worldwide descendants of Rajgród, we have raised the necessary funds and the sculpture is presently being shipped from Israel to Poland. A memorial ceremony in Rajgród will ensue upon the completion of this project.

ACKNOWLEDGEMENTS

Much love and gratitude to Galit Gottlieb my editor and dear friend. With her guidance, patience and expertise, she has helped bring my memoir into fruition.

Deep appreciation to my friend and teacher Lea Chapin, who has encouraged me to write my story and share it with the world. Her wisdom, insight and support has helped me to overcome some of the darkest moments of my life.

To Alisha, my soul sister: Thank you for your unconditional love and support. I am blessed to have you in my life.

To my dear cousins Jerry and Bella: Much appreication to both of you for sharing the untold stories of my family. These glimpses into the past might have otherwise been forgotten.

To my brother Barry: Your generousity has no limits. I am grateful beyond words. I love you.

To all my amazing friends: You are my chosen family. I am blessed to have each and everyone of you in my life.

To my ancestors: Grandmother Beila, Aunt Leah, Aunt Chaya, Aunt Josephine and all the martyred souls of Rajgród - You have not been forgotten. Your legacy lives on.

To Bobby: A kind, patient and loving soul. You are a true gentleman and the love of my life. I am beyond excited to be your wife!

To my mother, father and brother in spirit: A day never passes without thinking of you. I miss you and am comforted by your sense of presence in my life.

To Max, Noah and Raquel: You are my shining stars - my pride and joy - love you always and forever.

ABOUT THE AUTHOR

Karen Kaplan was born and raised in West Rogers Park, a Jewish neighborhood on the north side of Chicago. She received her B.A. from the University of Illinois in Chicago in Nutrition and Medical Dietetics. She also trained at The Claret Center of Hyde Park, Il. as a Spiritual Director. Karen maintained a private practice and lectured for many years throughout the Chicago metropolitan area on general health, weight loss, and spirituality.

After her father died, she began journaling memories (both bitter and sweet) that turned into a memoir of conquering the deep-seated fear and all-consuming hatred she felt towards him. Excerpts of her memoir were published in the Chicago Jewish News, The Patch, an online Chicago and suburban newspaper and the Landsmen, a publication for Jewish genealogists.

Raising her three children has been the most rewarding and joyous part of her life. Karen is currently engaged to Bob Weiss and lives in the Chicago area. A summer wedding is planned.

Painting by Linda Rubin Shayman
After Arie Kaplan witnessed his mother and two sisters pulled from their house and murdered by the mob, he ran into the forests of Eastern Europe and never returned home. His face in this painting seems lifeless and void of any happiness.The artist noticed a great resemblance between Arie and his daughter; so she painted the left half of the face as Arie and the right half as Karen.